Transforming
Ventures

Transforming Ventures

A Spiritual Guide for Volunteers in Mission

by
Jane P. Ives

UPPER ROOM BOOKS™
NASHVILLE

Transforming Ventures
A Spiritual Guide for Volunteers in Mission
Copyright © 2000 by Jane P. Ives
All rights reserved.

The Upper Room® Web site http://www.upperroom.org

Scripture quotations not otherwise identified are from the New Revised Standard Version of the Bible, copyright © 1989 by the Division of Christian Education, National Council of the Churches of Christ in the United States of America. Used by permission.

"This Is My Song." st. 1 by Lloyd Stone. © 1934, 1962 Lorenz Publishing Co. Reproduced by permission.

Cover design: Kym Whitley
Background cover transparency: Daryl Benson / Masterfile
Cover transparency: PhotoDisc
First printing: 2000

Library of Congress Cataloging-in-Publication Data

Ives, Jane P.
    Transforming ventures : a spiritual guide for volunteers in mission
/ Jane P. Ives
        p.   cm.
    Includes bibliographical references.
    ISBN 0-8358-0910-2
    1. Missionaries—Religious life. 2. Spiritual life—Methodist
authors. I. Title.
BV2063.I94   2000   99-32676
266—dc21   CIP

Printed in the United States of America

To my husband,
with whom I share the journey,
and to our children
and grandchildren,
that they may know God's
presence along the way.

Contents

Preface and Acknowledgments

WHILE LOOKING FORWARD to helping others, volunteers for short-term mission projects often do not foresee how involvement in mission endeavors may change their own lives. Experiencing a different culture, coming face to face with poverty and human need, and building Christian community with other team members can cause radical shifts in our understanding of God's work in our world. Persons unprepared for challenges to their worldview and self-perception may have difficulty responding positively and appropriating their learnings after returning home. This book, based both on my own experiences and on the reflections of other mission volunteers, offers guidance and resources to help volunteers in mission process the spiritually transforming aspects of their experiences.

My first work-team project took place in 1991. Six years earlier, a group from the United Methodist church my husband pastored in Maine went to northern Haiti to dig fishponds, an agricultural project designed to improve the food supply. Donald B. Small, a layman and mathematics professor, organized the trip. My husband, who had long dreamed of

During the night Paul had a vision: there stood a man of Macedonia pleading with him and saying, "Come over to Macedonia and help us."
—Acts 16:9

9

such a venture, joined the team, along with our college-aged son and daughter. I stayed home with our younger son, but the stories they told when they returned and the excitement in their eyes inspired my determination to take part in a similar trip someday.

Don Small decided to help establish a vocational school in one of the small, rural villages where the team worked. Every two or three years he returns to Haiti during his midwinter break to monitor and support its progress. In 1991, he organized a second work team to renovate a building at the vocational school to provide dormitory space for students who cannot commute. On the twenty-fifth day of December that year, my husband, our youngest son, and I undecorated our Christmas tree and stuck it in the snowbank outside our door. As we prepared to leave for Haiti early the next morning, I had no idea that this was only the first of many such trips; nor could I imagine how these ventures would impact my global understanding, self-awareness, and spiritual life.

Nine months after our return from Haiti, when we moved from Maine to West Virginia because of my husband's election to the episcopacy, we were thrilled to discover there a growing volunteer-in-mission program, spearheaded by the Reverend Tom Clark, but also energized by a number of other pastors and laypersons. Tom already had organized and led a number of teams to various sites across our country and to Jamaica, Mexico, and Nicaragua. He was eager to expand this program and excited by our enthusiastic support. My husband and I participated in the first West Virginia work team to Russia in the summer of 1994 and joined one of the three work teams our conference sent to Zimbabwe in 1997. In January of 1998, our educational tour of Israel included a work team extension in Jerusalem. Most recently we spent some time with a West Virginia team working at a barrio church in Mendoza, Argentina, and I participated with several other bishops' spouses in a trip to Kosovo organized by The United Methodist Committee on Relief. These ventures have altered my perspectives and stimulated in me an ongoing work of personal spiritual transformation. Working on this book has helped me process related insights and learnings, more fully comprehending and integrating the spiritual growth dimensions of these experiences.

The West Virginia Annual Conference of The United Methodist Church now sends out at least five teams a year to work on projects both within our country and abroad. In addition, many local churches send their own teams to work at mission sites within our conference or in other states. I want to thank Tom Clark, who to date has organized more than fifty-three international teams involving approximately nine hundred persons, for his leadership and for his encouragement of this book. Thanks also to Don Small, Monty Brown, and John Bowyer for their leadership of other mission work teams on which I have served. Thanks to the many team members with whom I participated in these adventures, especially those who have so graciously shared their thoughts and journals with me. I wish also to thank my editors George Donigian, who conceived this project and invited my participation, and Rita Collett, who so skillfully brought it to completion.

I owe deepest gratitude to my husband, with whom I share the journey in the fullest sense, for his encouragement and support of my mission ventures. We are grateful that our children, each having participated in one of these trips, can appreciate the significance and impact of our experiences.

Above all, thanks be to God for the ongoing journey and adventures of my life and for The United Methodist Church, which has nurtured me since childhood. My church connects me with brothers and sisters in Christ all over the world. Its Wesleyan heritage, which links personal spirituality with social concern, makes this book possible.

November 1999

How to Use This Guide

PART ONE: Before You Leave Home offers important insights, suggestions, and spiritual disciplines to prepare you for your mission project. Part Two: During Your Mission Project provides Bible study, reflection questions, and response suggestions for individual or team use while at your mission site. Part Three: After Your Return will help you process and integrate your new awareness and learnings when you come home.

To prepare for a mission project, complete Part One before you leave home. Use Part Two during your project, and work through Part Three after your return. If you have never gone on a mission trip and do not plan to do so soon, use your imagination to participate vicariously in these adventures. Perhaps you can use this guide to partner spiritually with mission volunteers you know, or perhaps it will inspire you to join a team. In any case you will find stimulus for personal growth and discover ways to be a mission volunteer at heart—in your daily life, in your church, and in your community—whether or not you ever travel geographically. If you have already participated in short-term mission

I am confident of this, that the one who began a good work among you will bring it to completion by the day of Jesus Christ.
—Philippians 1:6

projects, join me now in remembrance, celebration, and ongoing spiritual growth.

A Word to Team Leaders

As team leader, you will want to read this entire book before your mission trip, making note of your own experiences that further illustrate its themes and issues. Review the suggestions in the Resources section for group sessions before, during, and after your trip, as well as for commissioning services and other worship experiences. Encourage team members to complete Part One before leaving home, in addition to reading materials related to your particular project and destination.

Part Two provides materials for Bible study, reflection, and response while on-site. Individuals may use these on their own, but studying and discussing them together will enhance the impact for your team.

After your trip, some team members may take months or even years to complete Part Three. It is important that they thoroughly consider and assimilate these concepts rather than hurry through the material. Team reunions could provide an opportunity for members to share their use of Part Three. If it is impossible for the whole team to reconvene, perhaps small groups of persons who live near one another could meet occasionally or on a regular basis. You might even invite mission volunteers from different projects within the same church, community, or cooperative parish to meet for discussion and sharing of Part Three and to support one another in continued spiritual growth and mission.

Train yourself in godliness, for, while physical training is of some value, godliness is valuable in every way, holding promise for both the present life and the life to come. (1 Tim. 4:7-8)

Part One

Before You Leave Home

Orientation: A Team Convenes

NINETEEN OF US crowded into the meeting room of the airport restaurant, surrounded by our carry-on baggage and heaps of coats. Tom checked off the last name and smiled, calling us to attention.

"Good, we're all here. Welcome to the January work team for Africa University. We have a good number of veterans from former teams on this trip but some first timers too. We have a lot of ground to cover in the next two hours."

From around the room came murmurs of agreement. Tom nodded and continued, "Some of you don't know one another, so first let's go around the room, giving our names and the church we come from. Then share with us three things: Why are you going on this trip? What do you hope to give? And what do you hope to gain from the experience?"

The reasons and hopes came easily, some brief, others more detailed.

"I've heard what a spiritual blessing it is to go with the work teams, and I want to experience that."

"My lifelong dream is to go to Africa."

"To meet new people."

"To feel a sense of global unity."

Then I heard the voice of the Lord saying, "Whom shall I send, and who will go for us?" And I said, "Here am I; send me!"
—Isaiah 6:8

17

"This is my third trip to Africa. I look forward to taking part in the spiritual fervor of their worship again."

"You grow when you make the decision to be away from your family."

"To get out of my routines and have an adventure."

"I'm going to give all I can because I know I'll get more than I give."

Although I had participated in short-term mission projects before, I tasted anew the anticipation of a journey both outward and inward. Marveling humbly at the women who had come on their own, I smiled at my husband in gratitude for his making time to participate. Sponsored by the West Virginia Annual Conference of The United Methodist Church, our team included veterans of trips to Nicaragua, Mexico, and Russia, as well as several first timers. Leaders of conference mission agencies and United Methodist Women, including some who had traveled extensively, sat comfortably with local church members who had never before left the United States. Clergy and laity—grandmothers, young adults, and a high school senior—all were invited to address one another by our Christian names for the duration of this project, throughout which we would need to function as a team. Our mutual support and interdependence would shape the quality of our experience during the next two weeks.

Tom, our conference coordinator for short-term mission projects, zeroed in on the significance of our involvement. "These projects offer the most effective conversion experiences in the church today. The movers and shakers of the next century will come from other parts of the world. Christians are called to mission, but the church in the United States tends to be lazy and complacent. This hands-on experience will change your life if you let it, and hopefully you will want to share that experience with others when you return."

Tom then proceeded to remind us of necessary attitude adjustments. "We are going to work for and with others," he noted. "Things may not always be done our way."

One of the veterans laughed, "Yeah, remember when we were trying to build that doorway in Russia without a measure? I couldn't believe it when Yuri marked off a length of wood and shrugged, as if to say, 'Close enough.'"

"That's a good example," Tom nodded. "It's their project; we don't impose our standards on them. Which is not to say that we don't try to do our best, but they may have less to work with than we are used to; and the last thing we want to do is to sound critical or snobbish. Our real work is to be the face and hands of Jesus for people we don't even know yet and to see the face of Jesus in them. They are our brothers and sisters in Christ."

I remembered sadly how, during our work project in Haiti, one of the women in our group scornfully had dumped on the ground the contents of a glass that a Haitian woman had handed her. Of course it was not safe to drink, since it contained ice cubes probably made from untreated water. Some of the Haitians understood that our stomachs could not handle unfamiliar microbes, but others did not. Occasionally we had to pretend, expressing appreciation for refreshment we could not safely enjoy.

Tom moved the discussion along: "What have you learned from your reading?" Some of the team members recalled significant events from Zimbabwe's history. Others noted current problems and issues. "The more you understand of their experience," Tom said, "the easier it will be to 'walk in their shoes.' What cultural differences can you expect?"

"Well, the food will be different," someone suggested.

"They may be uncomfortable about females doing construction work," chimed in one of the older women. "In Russia they kept handing me a broom and telling me to 'tidy up,'" she laughed. "So I did, but I also spread cement every chance I got!"

"And the work pace! We had days in Russia when we could do no work because the materials hadn't been delivered."

"But we can't let that upset us," admonished Tom. "We Americans get really hung up on getting things done, but people in other countries value relationships and sociability more than productivity. It's not that one way is right and the other wrong. It's just different. Besides, we're spoiled, expecting things to go as we plan. People who are used to getting along with less don't get as bent out of shape about delays as we do."

"On my last trip, sometimes things didn't seem very sanitary," one of the women added, "but I adjusted and survived."

"Ah, yes," smiled Tom, "that's the key—adjustments! You may find yourself very uncomfortable at first, but give yourself a chance to adjust. You'll be surprised at yourself. And what are the three rules for work teams?" he grinned.

"Be flexible," shouted one of the veterans. "And number two is 'Be flexible,' and number three...." Several others chimed in, "Be flexible!"

Tom reminded us that our hand gesture for "okay" is considered an obscenity by some Africans and that at times our women would have to wear skirts and cover their arms in order not to offend. He advised us again of the importance of our functioning as a team and of the need for us to look out for one another at all times, making decisions with conscious awareness of the impact on others. After distributing assignment sheets for daily team devotions and for the team journal, he gathered us into a circle for prayer.

As we picked up our belongings and headed for our check-in gate, the words of a hymn from our commissioning service at annual conference echoed in my mind:

This is my song, O God of all the nations,
a song of peace for lands afar and mine.
This is my home, the country where my heart is;
here are my hopes, my dreams, my holy shrine;
but other hearts in other lands are beating
with hopes and dreams as true and high as mine.*

By faith Abraham obeyed when he was called to set out for a place that he was to receive as an inheritance; and he set out, not knowing where he was going. (Heb. 11:8)

*"This Is My Song." st. 1 by Lloyd Stone. © 1934, 1962 Lorenz Publishing Co. Reproduced by permission.

Preparation: Challenge and Opportunity

W HEN ASKED WHY she had signed up for the 1995 mission work team to Puerto Rico, Sookie Weymouth responded, "I was at a point in my life where I wanted to thank the church for all the love and support it gave me through my divorce and when I moved and had surgery afterwards. The church was like family to me, bringing in meals, providing transportation, packing and moving my belongings. You don't know how much you need others until you are alone! After my life stabilized, I started looking for ways to express my gratitude. When I learned about the Puerto Rico project scheduled during my vacation, it seemed meant to be!"

Sookie continued, "People asked why I was going so far away, when there is so much need right here at home. I explained that I do help others at home, but that I wanted to experience a different culture and try to change the negative impression of Americans held by many people in other countries. It wasn't easy to raise the $700 needed to participate, but I put on a

After this the Lord appointed seventy others and sent them on ahead of him in pairs to every town and place where he himself intended to go. He said to them, "The harvest is plentiful, but the laborers are few; therefore ask the Lord of the harvest to send out laborers into his harvest."

—Luke 10:1-2

lasagna dinner at the church and earned some of it. The mission committee at church helped with some of the rest. One team member asked for contributions from coworkers at her job, and another promised to send a postcard to those who contributed.

"As the time came closer," Sookie concluded, "I began to feel reluctant about going. My dog was sick, and I was just beginning a new relationship. But I had made the commitment and knew it was important not to back out."

Accepting the invitation to participate in a mission project often means leaving family and loved ones behind. Norma Denning describes this emotional challenge: "Even though we know we are in good hands, there's an underlying awareness, whenever I leave, that I might not come back. I have to consider how my family would function without me. That challenges me to get my house in order, not so much in terms of physical things, but more importantly in regard to relationships. Once when I was packing to go to Nicaragua, my son Sam asked if I was scared. I told him truthfully that I was, sort of, not so much that I might die, but that he might never know how much I love him. He grinned and hugged me, whispering, 'Sometimes I think the same thing.'"

Fear of flying, insecurity about the unknown, and dread of separation from loved ones can drain one's enthusiasm and energy as the date for departure draws near. Facing these anxieties straight on and placing our loved ones firmly in God's care can ease the stress. Carefully preparing for our time away can strengthen our confidence that we have made a good decision in signing up for this project. Thomas Moore in *The Re-Enchantment of Everyday Life* declares, "Travel gives rise to its own kind of spirituality: to a grand appreciation for community, to a passionate love of this earth, to an urgent longing for transcendence, and even to a sweet foretaste of death."[1] Difficult though it may be for us to rouse ourselves from our usual routines, doing so may open whole new dimensions of personal growth and understanding.

Before leaving for Mexico in 1992, Bill Miller remembered

John Wesley and Francis Asbury as they set out from England for their ministries in the New World. "I feel the same excitement of a new adventure they must have felt as they embarked for American shores and an unknown future, with the joyful anticipation of being able to share—or at least live out—the gospel across cultural barriers."

If we prayerfully surrender our illusion of control, if we embrace each day's opportunities for living in Christ's love and in right relationship with others, and if we surround ourselves with others who encourage and bless our venture, preparing to leave home can be rich and rewarding. Participating in team orientation meetings, reading about the area where we will be working, and praying both for our team members and for persons where we are going to serve—all help keep us focused forward into the experience. Mission team commissioning services, both during annual conference sessions and in local church worship settings, have blessed me with deep peace and an assurance of God's will for my life, confirmed by the supportive prayers of our church community.

On a practical level, of course, it is important to pack carefully and as lightly as possible. Some team leaders advocate a strategy learned from backpacking trips: Pack what you think you will need, and then remove half of it. Even so, we have sometimes experienced the embarrassment of dragging bulky luggage and wishing we were less encumbered. My husband once noted in his journal, "The Russians can't believe the amount of baggage that some of us are carrying. They live in small spaces, travel almost exclusively by public transportation, and know how to travel light." Deciding what you can get along without can be a spiritual discipline as well as a practical one!

However, do include gifts to share, small tokens of your home area and culture to give to persons you will meet. Crocheted or cross-stitched bookmarks, crafts made by you or others in your church, or postcards of your home area all convey a personal touch. Children everywhere appreciate pencils, pens, crayons, and paper. T-shirts or hats from local church or conference projects make both useful and meaningful gifts.

Most important of all, if you do not already journal as a regular practice, purchase or locate a journal and begin using it now! Although beautifully bound volumes with blank pages may be attractive, be sure that your choice tucks easily into your carry-on or backpack. Even a tablet or handful of composition paper will work if you make this journal a soul friend, confiding your deepest thoughts and feelings as well as details you want to remember. Date each entry and number the pages so that you can retrace your spiritual journey more easily.

Sally Campbell-Evans in *People, Places, and Partnerships* suggests using all your senses while traveling and upon arrival at your mission site, taking in everything around you. Write down in your journal the sights, sounds, and smells you experience while they are fresh in your mind. Describe persons you see and meet; record stories you hear; and jot down the correct spellings of names and places. Take notes on speeches and conversations, indicating the date, place, and names of persons involved. Write out your prayers of thanksgiving and concern. As you become more acclimated to your surroundings, you can begin to interpret and analyze both what you experience and your own reactions, questions, and feelings. Since the flood of new experiences may push things quickly out of short-term memory, you will want to keep your journal handy and update it often. Later when you reread what you have recorded, you may find recurring themes, changing perspectives, and deep personal insights that will help you process your spiritual journey.[2]

To open yourself most fully to God's transforming power throughout your mission project, begin now to record your responses to the Reflection questions and suggestions below and in each of the following theme chapters in Part One: Before You Leave Home.

"You did not choose me but I chose you. And I appointed you to go and bear fruit, fruit that will last, so that the Father will give you whatever you ask him in my name." (John 15:16)

Reflection

- What is your purpose for participating in this project? What moved you to sign up originally? Do you now experience other motivations?

- What fears might the seventy followers of Jesus have felt when he sent them out? What fears can you name as you prepare for this mission trip?

- Recall times in your life when you have known both fear and the presence of God empowering you through difficulties.

- What "unfinished business" do you leave behind in relationships and in your various involvements?

- How faithful have you been to prayer and other spiritual disciplines recently? Do you need to make a new or renewed effort to cultivate your relationship to God?

Response

- Prepare a list of those persons to whom you need to say loving words before you go. Make time to do so verbally, or write notes as necessary. As your departure draws near, confidently commend each of these persons to God's care. You may want to share with them this blessing:

  > The Lord bless you and keep you; the Lord make his face to shine upon you, and be gracious to you; the Lord lift up his countenance upon you, and give you peace. (Num. 6:24-26)

- List tasks that will need your attention when you return, and delegate responsibility to others wherever possible. As you record each task, release it, confident that if it fits God's purposes, it will in time get done.

- Contact persons who will pray for you during your trip. Tell them how much their prayers mean to you. Encourage those who are willing to partner with you in the use of this guide.

- Pray for the leaders and other members of your team by name, as well as for those persons who are preparing for your arrival. Thank God for their concern for your safety and comfort and for the way God is working in their lives.

- Envision your project completed, whether a building or an activity, and ask God's blessing on that vision.

- Read the eight theme chapters in Part One and use the suggestions for Reflection and Response to prepare yourself for the adventure ahead.

Prayer

Loving God, prepare me to serve you well in this venture. Ease my anxiety and fears and grant me courage to face the unknown. Help me sense your presence with me here and now, as well as ahead of me at our destination, making ready for our arrival. In the name of Jesus, who showed us how to trust in you. Amen.

"Go therefore and make disciples of all nations, baptizing them in the name of the Father and of the Son and of the Holy Spirit, and teaching them to obey everything that I have commanded you. And remember, I am with you always, to the end of the age."
(Matt. 28:19-20)

Theme 1

Discovering God Already at Work

I<small>N HIS BOOK</small> *Where in the World Is God?*, Robert Brizee responds to the question his title poses by affirming God's presence in every human event and experience. Brizee urges us to consider carefully which influences most likely come from God, amid the many we experience in each moment. We need to discern how God, rather than controlling, tries to persuade creation to evolve in harmony with divine purposes.[3]

When we moved to West Virginia in the fall of 1992, we began to explore different areas of the state. The contrast between the Wheeling area to the north and the southern West Virginia coal fields dramatized for me how geography (location and natural resources) and politics (decisions and actions of individuals and groups) work together to shape the history of a place. Although all of West Virginia is considered part of Appalachia, that notorious region of poverty and underdevelopment, distinct

"He has shown strength with his arm; he has scattered the proud in the thoughts of their hearts. He has brought down the powerful from their thrones, and lifted up the lowly; he has filled the hungry with good things, and sent the rich away empty."
—Luke 1:51-53

differences coexist within its borders. Along West Virginia's northern panhandle, the Ohio River flows south and west to the Mississippi, providing a transportation route, as well as a source of hydroelectric power. In the early years of our nation's history, the federal government established the National Road from the Potomac River near Cumberland, Maryland, to Wheeling and later across Ohio and Indiana into Illinois. Wheeling became a seaport and a jumping-off point for the developing West. Today the city hums with activity, its steel mills and power plants providing employment for a cosmopolitan population with all its attendant urban problems.

In contrast, southern West Virginia's geography consists of precipitous mountains interlaced with rivers and small "hollers." Here subsistence farmers and adventurous types moving west from the plantations of Virginia or south from settlements in Pennsylvania eked out a living from the land. The discovery of coal in these mountains unleashed a torrent of development activity. Coal barons and railroad owners contrived to wrest mineral rights from the tenants of these "hollers" and imported trainloads of laborers to work the mines. The shabby coal camps, busy for several decades, were abandoned when coal mining went high tech, rendering the huge labor force unnecessary. These pockets of poverty now seem to hold little hope for economic recovery. Even today, tax favors for out-of-state land and mine owners perpetuate the drain of West Virginia's natural resources and the suffering of its poor.

In both locations, mission projects address specific human problems related to unemployment, underemployment, and despair. Food pantries, clothing thrift shops, day care centers, housing rehabilitation, and economic development projects all seek to alleviate the pain of poverty and the hopelessness of people who feel excluded from the storied wealth of our country. God is at work in both of these areas, and God is made known through the love and courage of all, natives and newcomers and short-term mission volunteers, who rekindle hope while seeking to improve the quality of life.

With a deepened understanding of the interplay of geography and politics, I recalled our trip to Haiti in 1991. The rich resources of that beautiful land had been exploited and squandered by European conquerors, leaving its native people to scratch out a desperate existence. The erosion of barren hillsides, stripped of their mahogany trees for lumber to ship back to Europe, makes farming almost impossible. Military governments have controlled the citizens by terror and still threaten the populace, predominantly black descendants of Africans imported to work as slaves. Yet the people with whom we lived and worked during our stay demonstrated vital faith in spite of their hunger and their lack of adequate medical services and other benefits of modern civilization. Mission centers ministering to human need and working to reclaim the land nurture hope and bear witness to God's will for healing.

When we went to Russia in 1994, we found God at work there too, in startling contrast to our stereotyped image of this supposedly "godless" nation. In a small collective farm village southwest of Moscow, we found people who affirmed themselves as believers in spite of their suffering during the war with Germany, when their cities were destroyed and their rivers ran red with the blood of soldiers slain in brutal combat. Later, with the desecration of their beautiful cathedrals under the Stalinist regime, the faithful hid their icons and prayed in secret until recent developments freed them to worship publicly again.

While visiting Africa, we easily saw why European explorers coveted this land with its pleasant climate and generous space, recreating their culture and lifestyle in this tropical paradise. Although the conquerors used native peoples as laborers, they did not share equitably the benefits of their projects. Even today in Zimbabwe, although the native population has achieved liberation from white rule, Caucasians primarily of British descent still control most of the wealth. Yet mission schools, hospitals, and churches minister to human need. Vital congregations gather to worship, proclaiming faith in God's goodness despite their economic hardships.

If we affirm God's presence in every human event, we might wonder why suffering persists in so many places all over the world. In response to this question, Brizee asserts that God acts by persuasion rather than control.[4] Human selfishness often thwarts God's desire for beauty and harmony in creation. Yet God continuously calls us to make responsible and loving decisions, to serve as cocreators and healers, to transform the world by our actions and through our relationships.

"Your kingdom come. Your will be done, on earth as it is in heaven." *(Matt. 6:10)*

Reflection
- What stereotyped images do you hold of the places and people you will visit during your mission project?

Response
- Read about your destination's geography and history.
- Discover the natural resources with which God has gifted the area.
- Learn which decisions by groups and individuals have brought suffering to the area and which have brought blessing.

Prayer
Lord, I confess that I do not really know your children who live in the place where I will be serving you. Open my eyes, my ears, and my heart to understand what they have experienced and how you are working in their lives. Amen.

"The Spirit of the Lord is upon me,
because he has anointed me to bring good news to the poor.
He has sent me to proclaim release to the captives
and recovery of sight to the blind,
to let the oppressed go free,
to proclaim the year of the Lord's favor." (Luke 4:18-19)

Theme 2

Experiencing Hospitality

W<small>E ARRIVED IN</small> Baudin, a small village
in northwestern Haiti, on Frito's wedding
day in January 1991. Six years earlier,
when my husband and our college-aged
son and daughter came here to dig
fishponds, they met Frito, also in his early
twenties, and the rest of the Osias family.
His mother had since become lay leader
for their church, one of eight
congregations on a circuit served by a
pastor residing in nearby Cap-Haïtien.
This time our church in Maine sent a
team of eight, including our younger son,
then nineteen, to work on construction of
a dormitory for the vocational school.

Although we came prepared to sleep
on classroom floors, Madame Osias, a
slender, quiet-mannered woman, insisted
that we move into her home, a concrete
block structure approximately ten meters
square. The eight of us spread our sleeping
bags on the floor of the tiny rooms in the
back half of the house. She and her family,
the exact number of which we never did
discover, were to sleep in the other half. As
dusk fell, she brought us a gas lantern, the
only one in this remote village not yet

*So then you are no
longer strangers and
aliens, but you are
citizens with the
saints and also
members of the
household of God.*
—Ephesians 2:19

connected to the electrical lines several kilometers away. We followed her up the trail to the church for the wedding ceremony and joined in the festivities afterward at the elementary school next door. As I thought back to our older son's wedding two years earlier, I wondered how I would have reacted to the arrival of strangers from another world in the midst of our preparations and bustle.

Gracious hospitality embraced us again in Russia in 1994, when we traveled with a work team from West Virginia to Sitchi, a small rural collective farm village about two hundred kilometers south of Moscow. Neighbors dropped by the house that had been converted into a dorm for us, bringing fresh-picked raspberries and milk still warm from the cow. After a few days of working on housing construction, we received an invitation to a "barbecue in the forest." We really didn't know what to expect as we lurched over the rutted roads in an old blue bus, but shortly we arrived at a clearing in the woods at the edge of a field. There marinated pork sizzled on skewers over a blazing fire. We sang and relaxed while the feast was prepared, then gathered around a sheet of plastic on which our hosts had arranged plates and cups and tableware, fresh tomatoes, cucumbers, bread, and the savory meat. We feasted and then clapped and danced to the tunes of an accordion player, while the moon rose over hovering trees.

In January of 1997 while in Zimbabwe for work projects on the campus of Africa University, we attended a rural church set among glorious mountains. Although a bus delay brought us late to the service, several rows of empty seats awaited us in the front of the simple but spacious sanctuary. An interpreter told us what we had missed and guided our participation in worship, which was conducted in the Shona language. After the service our hosts invited us to stay for a reception for their new pastor. Church members brought a basin, a pitcher of warm water, and towels, holding them before each of us so we could wash our hands before soft drinks and cookies were served. Later we drank hot tea and ate freshly baked bread and butter sandwiches in the yard outside. Church members clustered about to chat with us, and children wrote down their addresses, urging us to find them pen pals or to write to them ourselves.

Not every work team initially receives such a warm welcome. Some who worked on a project in Nicaragua reported that it took most of their first visit to win the trust and friendship of the villagers there. Sadly, when we arrived in Sitchi, we found that we had to overcome a bad impression left by a previous group whose members had worked little and partied much. Generally, however, teams receive warm welcomes, and the hosts offer the best they can provide.

Some people feel more comfortable giving than receiving. Mission team participants, anticipating only what they have to offer, often find themselves unprepared for what may be the most important part of the experience. They may be overwhelmed by the generosity of those who seem to have less to share, amazed to discover that God has blessed even the very poor with loving hearts and thoughtful concern for others! If you feel uncomfortable receiving, you may need to prepare yourself to allow others the blessing of giving to you.

"Whenever you enter a town and its people welcome you, eat what is set before you; cure the sick who are there, and say to them, 'The kingdom of God has come near to you.'" (Luke 10:8-9)

Reflection

* Remember occasions when you have experienced the hospitality and generosity of others. How did you feel?

* What makes it difficult to accept hospitality from others? from those who seem less wealthy?

* Consider your own habits in relation to hospitality. How do you feel when company arrives unexpectedly? How do you feel about entertaining strangers?

- How would you like to respond in such situations? What makes it difficult for us to offer hospitality?

Response

- Imagine yourself and your family living as do your hosts, under the circumstances and in the conditions about which you have read. Now imagine that Christ has come to visit in the guise of a stranger. Consider how you might respond.

Prayer

Loving God, who taught us through your son that the sacrificial gift of the poor is more valuable than the easily given offering of the rich, free me from my tendency to judge and compare. Help me receive kindness and hospitality with gratitude. Bless all who prepare for our arrival and who concern themselves with our safety and comfort. Amen.

The point is this: the one who sows sparingly will also reap sparingly, and the one who sows bountifully will also reap bountifully. (2 Cor. 9:6)

Theme 3

Making Adjustments

OUR WORK TEAM arrived at Africa University sweaty and exhausted by long flights from Pittsburgh to London and from London to Harare, followed by a five-hour bus ride to Mutare. Imagine their dismay to discover that low water pressure restricted the availability of running water to an hour or so each morning and ten minutes each hour throughout the day. It was raining, however, and before long Tom was outside catching water from the drain spouts and offering shampoos to any one willing to lather up and rinse in cold water. Others quickly found plastic bags to fit over the spouts, emptying them into a plastic-lined garbage can as they filled. Men and women alike gathered by the brick drainage ditches, laughing and joking as they helped one another wash dust and oil from their heads and fatigue and disappointment from their hearts.

When my husband and I arrived, having stayed in Harare an extra day so he could preach at a local church there, enthusiasm bubbled over as our teammates described their inventive coping strategy. Eyes shone with the satisfaction of having

"Be strong and bold; have no fear or dread of them, because it is the Lord your God who goes with you; he will not fail you or forsake you."
—Deuteronomy 31:6

taken control of an uncomfortable situation, with joy in the bonding they had experienced, and with pleasure at the admiring cheers they received from passersby.

Short-term mission project journals abound with stories of persons who initially reacted to new situations with a desire to flee, but who, when encouraged and supported by their teammates, adjusted and discovered they could manage even what seemed intolerable. Some short-term mission volunteers do stay in comfortable hotels or dormitories, but differences in food, climate, and living conditions may still challenge their resourcefulness and adaptability. Unfamiliar food, heat and humidity, mosquitoes and flies, lack of comfortable beds, animal noises in the night and crowing roosters in the morning—all may disrupt sleep and cause physical distress. Although most of us prefer to avoid such circumstances, learning to adjust to different situations strengthens us and boosts our confidence.

Even apparently trivial improvements can lift morale by reestablishing a sense of control in uncomfortable situations. In Russia, Tom cheered us up by crafting a simple wooden toilet seat and toilet-paper holder and by placing a soda bottle filled with wild flowers in the dank, seatless privy. Coping strategies, like positive self-talk, mutual encouragement, and humor can also ease adjustments. Scriptural affirmations such as "I can do all things through him who strengthens me" (Phil. 4:13); breath prayers such as "Lord Jesus Christ, have mercy on me"; and hymns committed to memory can lift us above negative reactions and help us find inner peace and strength.

Packing small items to meet personal needs can help immensely. You may want to take along copies of pictures of loved ones, a prayer candle, or favorite devotional book; but don't pack precious things you would regret losing. Because our digestive systems get thrown off balance by irregular meal schedules, my husband and I always carry athletic energy bars. Persons with food allergies or intolerances may need to bring special crackers or infant soy powder to substitute for milk products. Packets of premoistened towelettes and antibacterial cleansers afford easy cleanup even when water is not readily available. Disposable tissues, hand lotion, hard candies or other small treats make life at a work site more pleasant. Be mindful, however, that it may not be easy to dispose of wrappers, containers, and other litter.

Most essential for adjusting to different living conditions is the recognition that our way of life is not an option for many in this world. Participating in a short-term mission project can impress upon us profoundly how much we take for granted and how much we fail to appreciate the blessings available to us.

No testing has overtaken you that is not common to everyone. God is faithful, and he will not let you be tested beyond your strength, but with the testing he will also provide the way out so that you may be able to endure it. (1 Cor. 10:13)

Reflection
* How do you usually respond to discomfort or inconvenience?
* What kinds of discomfort or inconvenience might cause you the most difficulty?
* What attitudes and spiritual disciplines have helped you cope in the past?
* What might you take with you to ease your adjustment?

Response
* Meditate on your possessions and mentally label them as *Necessities* or *Luxuries*. Which group is larger? What might that suggest about your lifestyle and values?
* As you pack, begin to simplify your expectations and needs by asking yourself, "Do I *really* need to take this?"
* Practice regularly a centering discipline to help you respond with spiritual power in every situation. Set aside a few minutes

each day in a quiet place. Still your body and your mind by breathing deeply. Visualize Jesus, using whatever image you prefer, surrounded by light. Sense both the brightness and the warmth of that light entering your body, perhaps through your head or the area of your heart. Choose a breath prayer or Bible verse or words of a hymn to accompany this discipline, such as one of the following:

Breathing in, say "Lord Jesus Christ"; breathing out, "grant me your peace."

"The Lord is my shepherd, I shall not want." (Ps. 23:1)

"Leaning, leaning, safe and secure from all alarms; leaning, leaning, leaning on the everlasting arms."[5]

Prayer

Lord, you have given me so much that sometimes I forget how little I really need in order to survive. I cling foolishly to things and comforts and forget that your grace is sufficient. Help me, as I venture into the unknown, to trust your love. In Jesus' name. Amen.

Surely God is my salvation;
I will trust, and will not be afraid,
for the Lord God is my strength and my might;
he has become my salvation.
(Isa. 12:2)

Theme 4

Liberating Time

THE PREACHER GLANCED anxiously at his watch as the van bounced over the rough dirt road. There was no way they could arrive by 10:00 A.M. for the scheduled service. In fact, it was almost noon when the driver announced, "Here we are!"

Gathering up his Bible and papers as he climbed out of the van, the preacher braced himself for disgruntled remarks from those who had waited. He was startled to hear instead cheers and happy greetings. He began to apologize for the delay but was silenced by protests, "No problem! We're just glad you're here."

In Kenya for the World Methodist Council in 1986, we first encountered a new sense of time, the conviction that an event is more important than the schedule and that people are more important than events. In Haiti, in Zimbabwe, yes, even in Russia, we could easily slip into complaining "ugly-American" style while waiting for the bus, for the phone call, for a promised arrival. We like things to happen on schedule, and we expect systems to be consumer friendly. Living in another culture can be a rude shock as we

For everything there is a season, and a time for every matter under heaven.
—*Ecclesiastes 3:1*

discover how spoiled we have become. When people struggle against great odds just to survive, a few hours' wait here and there seems insignificant. Perhaps an inflated sense of our own importance and of the power we feel we should exert over others creates such impatience in us.

Raymond K. DeHainaut, in an article on cross-cultural spirituality, addresses these differences in attitudes toward time: "We need to practice patience when we experience the manner in which some cultures—such as Arab, African, or Latin—manage time. In many cultures, arriving ten minutes to an hour late for an appointment is no cause for alarm. There is greater tolerance for tardiness, and the announced time for an event is not taken too seriously."[6] Instead of rushing to get down to business, people of other cultures place a higher value on warm personal relationships.

In contrast, our busy-ness, which Thomas Moore labels "a neurotic development of modern life," leaves many of us thinking we don't have time to enjoy nature and relationships.[7] Indeed, I struggle constantly with my "overactive responsibility gland," my need for accomplishment, my tendency to schedule more for the day than I can reasonably complete. I seem to have to go halfway around the world and immerse myself in another culture in order just to "hang out."

It is not that people in other countries have little to do. At Africa University we met a young mother who walks three hours from her village home to her job on campus every morning. After six hours of cleaning the dormitories and doing laundry for students, she walks back to her home, sometimes knitting along the way. She hopes soon to enroll in evening courses to pursue her education. Bill Miller, journaling during a work experience in Mexico, noted, "Most people here earn their living by farming or grazing livestock. Many also work for the electric company. They work from 6:00 A.M. until evening and are paid very little. In fact, the stereotype of a lazy Mexican spending the day sleeping in front of a building with a sombrero over his eyes is totally inaccurate. They do hard physical work from dawn until after dark with little to show for it. Lacking a welfare system, they rely on hard work and teamwork to survive. The children are all beautiful and very friendly, though they too must work. I have seen children about six years old shepherding large flocks of sheep and cows all alone."

Yet, Bill continues, in spite of their heavy work loads, "Mexicans spend evenings the way evenings ought to be spent. They sit around talking as families—about everything. The kids play games outside, running in every once in a while to grab some food or to sit on your lap, before running out again. They play the games of my childhood, like hopscotch, tag, and anything else your imagination might create. They do not have toys, video games, or TV to stifle their imaginations. The adults, likewise, visit and talk, hang around and snack, the way people in our country used to."

One of the basic tenets of religious practice for the ancient Hebrews was the observance of Sabbath time. Orthodox Jews and some Christian groups today continue to set aside blocks of time they consider sacred, designated for rest and renewal. In Hebrew tradition, the Sabbath begins at sundown Friday evening and continues until sunset on Saturday. Christians, who celebrate the resurrection of Christ on Sunday, sometimes blur these two observances together. Earlier this century, many Christian homes honored strict prohibitions against playing cards, going to movies, or shopping on Sunday. With extended store hours and the expansion of tasks on the modern family's "to-do" list, the concept of Sabbath is easily lost. Yet if we do not take time for renewal, rest, and play on a regular basis, we cannot effectively fulfill our covenants with others. Observing some Sabbath time each day, each week, each month, and each year can prevent burnout and empower us both in our relationships and in our work.

"And can any of you by worrying add a single hour to your span of life?" (Matt. 6:27)

Reflection

- What is your usual attitude toward time? How important are schedules and promptness?

- In what kinds of situations are you most impatient?

- For what activities do you wish you had more time?

- To what extent do you observe the Sabbath, as described in Exodus 20:8-11?

Response

- Even though—or maybe especially because—you are busy preparing for your trip, take some time to sit quietly by yourself and think about what is most important in your life. List your priorities on a page in your journal.

- Make time for relaxed conversation and simply being with those persons most dear to you. Listen actively to what they say, assuring them of the value you place on their feelings and experiences.

- Continue to practice your centering discipline at least daily but more often when you feel hurried or pressured by things you think you need to do. Add the following scripture verse to those you already use to calm and focus yourself: "This is the day that the Lord has made; let us rejoice and be glad in it" (Ps. 118:24). You might find the musical version even easier to recall, a lyrical affirmation for beginning the day or for dealing with your own impatience as needed.[8]

Prayer

Lord of all time and of every moment in my life, empower me constantly to seek your will and your purpose. And, O Lord, grant me patience and trust to do what you would have me do and to be what you would have me be. In the name of Jesus. Amen.

Take my moments and my days;
let them flow in ceaseless praise.[9]

Theme 5

Meeting Jesus

W<small>HEN WE ENTERED</small> the orphanage at Old Mutare Mission, across the road from Africa University, the children who clustered in the doorway overwhelmed us, reaching for hugs and jumping up and down with excitement. While others on our team worked on faculty housing or book processing in the library, five of us came to play with the children and help feed them lunch. Here in the "Babyfold," two daily shifts of four women do all the cooking, feeding, bathing, dressing, diapering, laundry, and cleaning for thirty or so abandoned and orphaned children. These workers do a good job with limited resources, but the children know that visitors can give them more hugs and attention. We found ourselves trying to hug and carry, while simultaneously protecting our glasses, watches, hair, and clothing from the eager grasps of giggling, shrieking children. Sometimes we succeeded in organizing a game of tag or London Bridge or ball tossing, but eventually we just sat and let the children climb over us, savoring the short-lived peace when one or another snuggled for a quiet moment.

Have we not all
one father?
Has not one God
created us?
—Malachi 2:10

43

Although little children tug at the hearts of visitors with special poignancy, perhaps because they seem so vulnerable, mission volunteers make friends of all ages and sizes. Africa University students from Angola, Liberia, Sierra Leone, and other nations, unable to go home for the midwinter break because of the distance from—or warfare in—their homelands, invited our team to meet with them for an evening of fun and sharing. They sat with us at meals and chatted eagerly about their families, their hopes and dreams, and their problems. In Haiti, several young men who helped with the dormitory renovation came to us in the evening, begging for English lessons and enthusiastically practicing the phrases we taught them. Our Russian interpreters, three young college students on summer vacation, expressed amazement that Americans would come to live in a remote farming village. They participated in our team meetings and joined in our work and play. One afternoon in a Russian marketplace, an old woman selling dried beans approached us curiously. With the help of our interpreter, we explained where we came from and shared information about our children and grandchildren. The woman grinned gleefully, declaring surprise that we were not "mean" like the Americans she had seen portrayed on Russian television programs.

Discovering how much we have in common with people from very different circumstances helps break through stereotypes and shatter the illusion that we are entirely unique. Youth from The United Methodist Church in Lubeck, West Virginia, reflecting on their work experience in Washington, D.C., spoke admiringly of the collegial way staff persons related to those who came regularly to Zacchaeus' Kitchen. Meghann confessed that when she ate in the soup kitchen before beginning work there, she found herself wanting to cling to her friends. She had to overcome her fears and personal reluctance in order to relate to those who came out of need. For members of the group who have always lived in white rural areas, this trip provided their first in-depth encounter with African-Americans. As a result, Nathan affirmed he no longer reacts to black people with automatic fear and distrust. Ashley expressed her surprise: "Seeing how alike we are made me realize how much we just take for granted or think we deserve."

Their seminar leader, reported Margot, admonished them always to look people in the eyes, to recognize them as fellow human beings, even if declining a request for a handout. Her advice echoes John Wesley, who noted that the word translated as "visit" in Matthew 25:36 more accurately means "look upon." When Jesus states the importance of visiting the sick, he is in fact exhorting us to be "present with" and look upon them with our own eyes. Wesley broadened this teaching by including "all such as are in a state of affliction, whether of mind or body;...whether they are good or bad, whether they fear God or not." He continues, "To send them assistance is therefore entirely a different thing from visiting them. The former then ought to be done, but the latter not left undone....One great reason why the rich in general have so little sympathy for the poor is because they so seldom visit them."[10]

Likewise Ambrose Reeves, bishop of Johannesburg, South Africa, declared in 1965, "In every genuine human encounter with another person we may become aware of Jesus, and meet with him....Jesus himself showed that for this to happen demands courage and a willingness to move from a life that is centered in itself."[11] More recently, Mother Teresa in *No Greater Love* expanded on this theme of meeting Jesus in our encounters with others, especially the poor:

There is a man standing there on the corner, and you go to him. Maybe he resents you, but you are there, and that presence is there. You must radiate that presence that is within you, in the way you address that man with love and respect. Why? Because you believe that is Jesus....He comes disguised in the form of that person there. Jesus, in the least of His brethren, is not only hungry for a piece of bread, but hungry for love, to be known, to be taken into account.[12]

During Carter Crawford's first day working on church construction in Nicaragua, a lady came running out of her house, screaming at the white people to go home. However, at the end of two weeks, when the team had finished their work, she cried openly as they said their good-byes. Another time, when Carter and his wife Ruie worked in a poor black church in South Carolina, hugs and blessings were shared at the end of a worship service. A small black woman, probably eighty years old, said to Carter, "I've never hugged a white man before." Carter laughed and promptly declared, "Well then, we better do it again!" Such encounters, says Ruie, are what keep them motivated to continue serving as volunteers. Now retired, they use their recreational vehicle to travel to mission sites within our country through the United Methodist NOMADS program, as well as joining international teams whenever possible.

When Jim McCune and Tom Clark traveled to Moscow in the spring of 1998 to prepare to bring a team there in July, a remarkable encounter dramatized the power of Christian love in cross-cultural relationships. Jim, a United Methodist campus pastor at Marshall University in Huntington, West Virginia, reports, "I had always believed that 'the world is my parish' but had never had that philosophy cut so deeply into my heart and mind until we came to the orphanage in Sergiyev Posad. It was there that I saw the devotion of nurses caring for infants and children, perhaps victims of fetal alcohol syndrome, perhaps Chernobyl. Their devotion to these children (for a meager $30 per month) was a great witness of the human spirit of compassion. Humbled by the staff's steady and disciplined care for these children, I was even more touched by the joy the children expressed upon seeing us. A young girl, perhaps twelve years old, took my hand with great intention and led me up a long hallway. While a little boy who followed her echoed every word, she pointed out storybook characters displayed in picture frames on the wall. She told me the Russian name, and I responded with the English name. Although I did not understand her language, one word came through clearly.

With great longing in her eyes, her head turned to the side, she looked at me and said with that distinctive roll of the tongue, 'Brent?' I knew immediately that she was inquiring about Brent Brown, who had brought West Virginia teams to Sergiyev Posad the past two summers. Looking at this little girl and the tiny boy in her shadow, I simply said the Russian word for July. Remembering the excitement on their faces when they heard my reply still brings tears to my eyes."

"Then the righteous will answer him, 'Lord, when was it that we saw you hungry and gave you food, or thirsty and gave you something to drink? And when was it that we saw you a stranger and welcomed you, or naked and gave you clothing? And when was it that we saw you sick or in prison and visited you?'" (Matt. 25:37-39)

Reflection
- How do you usually respond to persons who seem different from yourself?
- What feelings do you have?
- Are you more comfortable with children or adults?
- When and where have you discovered what you have in common with persons from different circumstances?

Response
- Continue practicing your centering discipline.
- Pray the Lord's Prayer as Jesus taught his disciples (Matt. 6:9-13), emphasizing the very first word.
- When you pass strangers on the street, look at them, make eye contact, and acknowledge the divine spark within each person.

- Read about your mission site, looking for information about culturally acceptable behaviors. For example, some places consider eye contact disrespectful. Some of our common gestures convey different and even insulting meanings in other cultures.

- Monitor your thoughts about other persons, correcting any tendency to judge those whose experiences you do not understand.

- Pray for those persons who will host you at the mission site and for the new friends you will meet there. Thank God for what is happening in their lives and for the changes already taking place in your attitudes and feelings.

Prayer

Dear Lord and Creator of all humankind, help me see beyond surface differences to the essential core, the spark of divine, in everyone I meet today. In the name and love of Jesus. Amen.

"And the king will answer them, 'Truly I tell you, just as you did it to one of the least of these who are members of my family, you did it to me.'" (Matt. 25:40)

Theme 6

Building a Team

"BEFORE OUR TRIP to Africa University," confessed Clara Belle Denning, "many questions haunted me. Would I be able to keep up with the others, given my physical condition and difficulty with walking? What work could I do? If I couldn't pull my share of the load, would the rest of the team accept me? Would I be just a 'fifth wheel'? These concerns were soon put to rest. Even though there was a wide age difference among our team members, everyone seemed to affirm the variety of interests and abilities, gifts and graces. No one seemed to worry about whether we all had the right skills and qualifications to serve on the team. We quickly became a family, respecting, helping, and encouraging one another."

Judy Jerman grinned and agreed. "God seems to put the right people together. I don't know anything about housing construction and couldn't imagine what I would do. When we went to the orphanage, it felt like a place just waiting for me." Judy, along with several other members of the team, returned to the orphanage every day. Clara Belle and

For as in one body we have many members, and not all the members have the same function, so we, who are many, are one body in Christ, and individually we are members one of another. We have gifts that differ according to the grace given to us ....Let love be genuine; hate what is evil, hold fast to what is good; love one another with mutual affection; outdo one another in showing honor.
—Romans 12:4-6, 9-10

49

Bonnie, in addition to processing books for the library, borrowed a sewing machine and helped the orphanage seamstress by making children's clothing, as well as aprons for the staff. Lessie became a plastering expert, working alongside those with construction experience and skills. Indeed, everyone's gifts were affirmed and put to good use.

Similarly, Sookie described the team with which she traveled to Puerto Rico. "Our group included teenagers and an eighty-year-old and others in between, and there were other amazing differences as well. One retired man practically supervised the construction project, while his wife did laundry and liaison work. She visited with the staff and residents at the nursing home, smiling, making conversation, and demonstrating care for persons. Some of the younger team members made friends with Puerto Ricans and visited in their homes. They learned much and were able to share with the rest of us details about individuals and life in this village. I was assigned to cook because of my experience but enjoyed helping with construction too. I especially liked doing things by hand the old-fashioned way, not depending on machines."

Participation by all members in a variety of tasks enhances the group life of a team and the sense of belonging for individuals. Laypersons, as well as clergy, can lead devotions and offer table graces or prayer before starting a project or journey. Team members may rotate many responsibilities, such as counting heads to be sure all are present or checking for litter when leaving an area. Some teams assign a different individual to record each day's events in a team journal, which often includes hilarious jests and exaggerations. Norma Denning typed up the entries after our trip to Africa University and sent us each a copy, complete with pictures, capturing the particular flavor and events of our time together. Work team projects afford many opportunities for participants to use their various gifts and perhaps even to discover gifts they didn't know they had.

While many team leaders require participation in orientation and training sessions before mission trips, Tom Clark does not. "When people who do not know one another have several occasions to gather before their trip, they often begin to form cliques or to find fault with other team members," he says. "Such judgments may be processed and ingrained over the weeks and months before the work team experience. I prefer to do most of the orientation through mailings and phone conversations, keeping participants' personalities a mystery until the day of departure or in some cases the night before. When they gather for a two- or three-hour orientation just before the two-week experience, generally a wonderful sense of discovery adds to the mystical experience of the work team. That charges the atmosphere with excitement, providing a good opportunity for team members to bond, with the knowledge that they will be together for a set period of time. There will be plenty of occasions for team members to rub each other the wrong way, but almost anything and anyone can be tolerated for two weeks, especially when there is no easy escape from the work team site, and you can't just decide to take your ball and go home when things don't go your way."

Perhaps the most challenging aspect of being on a team is learning to make decisions based on the probable consequences for all, not just for oneself. Individuals who stray from the group in order to do their "own thing," who fail to take reasonable care of their health, or who ignore group rules can cause problems for the entire team. In Moscow a member of our work team accidentally was separated from the rest of his group. He made his own way back to the hotel, rather than waiting in place as instructed. The rest of his group spent hours looking for him, generating considerable worry and stress! When team members are ill or injured, the whole team may need to adjust its plans, and usually members do so willingly and graciously. An illness or injury resulting from carelessness, however, presents unnecessary inconvenience and may well cause resentment and anger. Team members may need frequent reminders to stop and think about their responsibility for the well-being and productivity of the whole group.

Intentional work teams nurture their group life by setting aside time each day for worship and for processing their experiences. Sookie's team began the morning with devotions, led by a different team member each day, then used their evening mealtime for in-depth sharing and planning for the next day. Other teams gather in the evening for sharing and devotions. In addition to checking in with individuals from time to time to see how things are going, sensitive team leaders create an accepting, loving group atmosphere in which members can express their feelings and needs. Team meetings provide an opportunity for members to request changes in their task assignments, to ask for help with whatever may be troubling them, and to appeal for prayer support. These sessions can take on the flavor of John Wesley's class meetings as members ask one another, in whatever words may be comfortable, "How is it with your soul?"

Near the end of a team's experience, Tom Clark affirms the uniqueness of their ministry and points out that they already have left something of themselves at their project site, which they may never get to visit again. He suggests that they each leave something symbolic of their presence, perhaps a calling card or photo or personal note, hidden at the site. Anne Carpenter describes how her work team, after helping rebuild a South Carolina church burned by an arsonist, left a letter and a small white Bible inscribed with the date and all their names sealed in a plastic bag nailed to the wall studs behind some sheet rock in the sanctuary. "I showed some of the children in the congregation where we had put the package, asking them to tell their grandchildren about the people from West Virginia who had come to help rebuild their church and who had left a message for future generations." Such rituals dramatically symbolize the meaning of an experience, providing common memories and lifelong connections for team members.

Now there are varieties of gifts, but the same Spirit; and there are varieties of services, but the same Lord; and there are varieties of activities, but it is the same God who activates all of them in everyone. (1 Cor. 12:4-6)

Reflection

- Recall other experiences of working with a team, perhaps in sports, in church, on committees, or as part of your job. What do you like about being part of a team?

- What do you find difficult?

- What gifts and graces, interests, and abilities do you bring to your work team?

- What gifts and graces, interests, and abilities do you hope others will bring?

Response

- Continue your centering discipline at least daily and additionally in situations that require you to work cooperatively with others. Seek God's direction both for the role you are to play and for ways you can support others.

- If you already know any of those who will be on your team, avoid assuming you know what they will be like during your project.

- Pray for your team members by name, invoking God's power in their lives as they prepare for the project in which you will participate together.

Prayer

Gracious God, help me move beyond selfish preoccupations to think of myself as part of this team. Keep me mindful of the needs of others and willing to do more than what I usually consider to be my share. In the name of Jesus Christ. Amen.

Part One

If then there is any encouragement in Christ, any consolation from love, any sharing in the Spirit, any compassion and sympathy, make my joy complete: be of the same mind, having the same love, being in full accord and of one mind. Do nothing from selfish ambition or conceit, but in humility regard others as better than yourselves. Let each of you look not to your own interests, but to the interests of others. (Phil. 2:1-4)

Singing the Lord's Song

Wₕₑₙ ᴍʏ ʜᴜsʙᴀɴᴅ returned from his first trip to Haiti, he described one of the highlights of that experience, an evening worship service held at a nearby crossroads. "Frito took us to a prayer meeting about a five-minute walk from the village center. We walked through several yards and between the huts, then down a narrow rutted lane until we reached the place where it met the dirt road. About fifty or sixty Haitians, including a number of children, gathered around a table that had been set in the center of the intersection. On it stood the village's only gas lantern. Frito insisted on getting us some chairs, even though most of the Haitians were standing or sitting on the ground. The service consisted of scripture reading and songs, some solos and duets and numbers by the youth group, and sometimes the whole group singing together. We joined in the songs we knew and sang a couple hymns for them. Don responded to their words of greeting. Frito translated for us and kept us up-to-date on what was happening,

How could we sing
the Lord's song
in a foreign land?
—Psalm 137:4

even finding the scripture readings for us in an English Bible he had brought along, so that we could follow the text. During the service, which lasted about two hours, walkers and bicycle traffic passed along the road, but we continued to sing and pray and shout 'Amen.'"

Sookie smiled as she recalled Sunday worship in Puerto Rico. "It was all in Spanish, filled with music accompanied by drums and guitars. No hymn books; they just knew the songs....The children moved freely about and were welcomed and loved by everyone. When they got hungry, they were fed a cooked cereal. Teenaged boys and girls made eyes at each other. A woman went up to the altar rail and swooned, but no one seemed alarmed."

Bill Miller describes a similar experience in Mexico: "The evening Communion service lasted two hours, about half of it with us all standing up. It was a great experience, even though we couldn't understand most of it. We felt very privileged and followed the service in the old hymnals. Every seat was filled, with a congregation of at least sixty. The most touching part of the service is that all the children come to the altar first. Twenty of them came up to receive Communion with their parents. Their amazingly good behavior demonstrated what I have observed to be a generally respectful relationship between children and parents. These people are so devout. They worship morning and evening at church, as jobs permit. They pray at every meal. They love to sing religious music. All their celebrations, including weddings and birthdays, are religious in content."

In addition to such lively and rich worship experiences, participants in volunteer mission projects may also discover the deep faith reflected in the personal family devotions of their hosts. In the early morning darkness, after our first night sleeping on the floor in Madame Osias's house during our visit in Haiti, we were wakened by the sound of a match striking in another room and the flare of light reflected on open roof beams above. The voices of the Osias family, joined in murmured prayers and responses, touched us deeply and soothed the disorientation we felt upon waking in a strange place.

Like the Hebrews exiled in Babylon, we may wonder how we will worship God in a foreign place. Unlike the Hebrews, however, we probably will find ourselves among fellow believers, whose joy in worship, expressions of praise and faith, and desire to serve Christ may prompt twinges of shame at our own spiritual laziness. Large choirs, accompanied by drums and tambourines and singing with rhythmic energy, and happy congregations participating enthusiastically in song and prayer and mutual greeting—all may make some of our home church services seem tame! The more formal Russian Orthodox churches, with their elaborate rituals and decor, their ancient icons, arouse in us a sense of timelessness and mystery. We feel connected to the early followers of Christ, as well as to those who lived through the painful years when they had to hide their faith from an oppressive government.

While waiting in Moscow for some late-arriving team members, Tom happened upon a small Russian Orthodox church at one end of Red Square. Intrigued by the beautiful chanting, he went inside and discovered a worship service in progress. He asked his guide to explain some of the rituals, specifically the abundance of candles in every part of the sanctuary. She explained that the candles were placed there by individuals offering prayers, some for thanksgiving, some for healing, some in praise of God. Tom purchased a candle for each member of his family, all left behind in West Virginia. He lit one of them with prayers for the healing of his twenty-one-year-old daughter, who recently had been diagnosed with a brain tumor. "Four years and one additional surgery later," he reports, "she is healthy and whole, as is the new grandson she has presented to us. I remember gratefully a new expression of faith made available to me in that little cathedral on the corner of Red Square."

Unique aspects of a team's experience may inspire and enrich its worship life. Returning from his first trip to Haiti on a DC-3, my husband huddled with the rest of the team in the cargo area and served Communion, using a small can of grape juice and some crackers. While in Russia, we celebrated the sacrament in the front yard of our farmhouse dormitory, using cold tea and homemade bread from the village store. Several villagers stopped by to share in the service with us, identifying themselves through our interpreters with the words, "We are believers." A team in Mexico sat on the cement block walls of the church building they had started to construct and received the elements, juice served in a styrofoam cup and fresh bread from the market. They had spent two weeks digging, building the footer, and setting in place only four layers of the cement blocks. Although they found it hard to leave the unfinished project, this service of Holy Communion affirmed their connection both to those who had made this project possible and to those who would come later to finish it.

During our evening team meetings in Russia, we responded to memories of the day lifted up by individual members with a unison response, "Praise be to God." One of our young Russian interpreters, when asked how she felt about these informal services of praise and prayer, commented, "I feel warm all over, and I don't know why." Work team members may experience many heart-warming moments as they participate in indigenous church services, worship with one another in group gatherings, and privately practice their own spiritual disciplines.

Rejoice always, pray without ceasing, give thanks in all circumstances; for this is the will of God in Christ Jesus for you. (1 Thess. 5:16-18)

Reflection
* What experiences of worship have you shared in settings other than your own community of faith?
* How would you describe the worship life of your church? In what ways does this style of worship satisfy you? satisfy others in the congregation?

- What personal and family devotional practices did you experience growing up?

- What personal spiritual disciplines do you practice? Are you satisfied with these? Have you considered changing them or trying something new?

Response

- Continue your centering discipline, at least daily. You may also find it a helpful way to "tune in" spiritually during group worship services and in church.

- If you do not already do so, try approaching different parts of your day with specific prayers. Upon awakening, joyfully receive the new day and ask God's direction in all your activities. Express gratitude for every good gift, including food, glimpses of beauty, pleasant encounters. When troubled or uncertain, affirm God's presence and guidance. At the end of the day, again give thanks, acknowledging and letting go of what has not gone well and placing yourself in God's healing care during your hours of rest.

- Consider taking along on your trip some worship resources, such as song sheets, prayers, or litanies to share with others on your team and with new friends at your mission site.

Prayer

Almighty Creator God, your goodness and power are beyond my comprehension. For every blessing—large and small, known and unknown—I give you thanks and praise. I ask your continued blessing and guidance that I may truly serve you in this world. In Jesus' holy name. Amen.

Draw near to God, and [God] will draw near to you.
(James 4:8)

Theme 8

Maturing in Christ

RICHARD WORK, recently named Hunger Coordinator of the Year by The United Methodist Committee on Relief, described to me his initial experience as a mission volunteer. While attending seminary in Atlanta, he served as youth pastor at a large, multiple-staff church. The youth there had previously participated in a mission trip through Appalachia Service Project, Inc., and were preparing for a second trip to southern West Virginia. A native of New Jersey, Richard had completed his undergraduate studies at West Virginia Wesleyan and looked forward to returning to this beautiful state.

The work team consisted of thirty-five youth and adults, some veterans of the previous project and other first timers, most of them very well off financially. Richard commented, "Those youth had just about everything they wanted, and I guess I did too. My wife had a good job, and with my church position we were probably better off than most other seminary students. My group was sent to a house that was so run down it was unlivable. The family dropped by to see

For the creation waits with eager longing for the revealing of the children of God; for the creation was subjected to futility...in hope that the creation itself will be set free from its bondage to decay and will obtain the freedom of the glory of the children of God.
—Romans 8:19-21

how the work was progressing, and some neighborhood children came by from time to time. Otherwise we were rather isolated—our attitude was pretty much 'them' and 'us.'"

"Actually our group had a terrible attitude," Richard continued. "We kept to ourselves and complained constantly—about the food, about the living conditions, about having to go across the street to ask if we could use someone's bathroom. We were really working hard. One girl spilled paint on a horsehair pad, which we didn't realize the family used for a rug. The staff berated us for this carelessness, and we felt sorry for ourselves. One girl asked, 'Why are we doing this if it's so awful?'"

Richard leaned forward and continued earnestly, "Suddenly we experienced what I can only call a Holy Spirit moment. Someone asked, 'If we can't give of ourselves, remove ourselves from being comfortable for one week, then what is our faith about, what does it say about us? Have we no gratitude for all we have?' In preparation for the devotions our group was to lead at Friday's team meeting, we had chosen the song 'Hammer and a Nail' by the Indigo Girls from Atlanta. It crystallized what we were beginning to understand about serving Jesus through our labors, about allowing your spirit to work as well as your hands. Our group's attitude became so transformed that when we retiled the family's kitchen floor, working with the assortment of unmatched tiles that had been provided, the youth would not settle for random placement but struggled until they created a pattern. The family, apparently not used to having people really invest in them, expressed amazement at this effort. When we sang our song during Friday's devotions, we could not contain our emotions.

"I still keep a picture of that group in my office," Richard said, pointing it out to me, "and I try to stay in touch with them. We were so bonded by this experience. It had a lasting effect on me. Whenever I catch myself complaining; when I allow myself to take privileges for granted, to be arrogant and ungrateful, the memory of that Holy Spirit moment breaks in on me, sometimes through words from that song."

Mission work projects can bring out both the best and the worst in each of us, causing us to face our weaknesses and opening us to new possibilities for personal growth. Thrown into a different cultural setting, living in close proximity with persons we may not have known before, stripped of our usual sources of security and comfort, we may find ourselves vulnerable and our defenses weakened. We may become irritable, tense, and impatient. It's important to be aware of how and what we are feeling. Sookie Weymouth, sharing a bunk room with other women, found herself challenged by the lack of privacy or personal space. "I learned that I am more of an introvert than I thought. I really need time to myself. It helped to go for a walk now and then, sometimes with a really good friend who shared the same feelings of frustration." Recognizing and owning our needs frees us to find creative ways to honor them.

During work team projects, as well as whenever I feel particularly stressed, I sometimes struggle with demons I thought I had already conquered, namely self-centeredness and the longing to be loved. Hannah Hurnard, the author of *Hinds' Feet on High Places*, likens this longing to a deep-rooted plant that must be torn out of our hearts to make room for unselfish love to grow.[13] My hunger for affirmation can blind me to the needs of others. When I am full of myself, I have no room for God or for other persons. Competitiveness, which I know to be rooted in low self-esteem, sometimes creeps up within me. When my sense of self-worth is depleted, I tend to look around at others to judge and compare, to see if I can at least feel equal, or even superior, to someone else. Recognizing the folly of such thoughts just adds guilt to the mix. At such times I need to embrace the hurting child within me, forgive her for this foolishness, and remind her of the good news that all are precious in God's sight. It helps to find an understanding friend or small group to do that for me! It also helps to recognize where such patterns came from, to forgive parents or significant others who may have modeled them for us, and to own the life questions that haunt and challenge us.

Someone has written that our weaknesses may simply be our strengths taken to extremes. Certainly my organizational skills can slide over into compulsion, my creativity into perfectionism, my concern for persons into a tendency to control. Keith Miller, in *A Hunger for Healing*, claims that spirituality involves being in touch with reality—"one's own reality and feelings, the reality of other people, and ultimate reality, which is God and [God']s will." The purpose of spiritual disciplines, then, is "to face, discover, and let God remove the character defects that distort our perception of reality and of God and ruin our lives and relationships."[14] Mission work projects provide an excellent setting for such self-discovery and for experiencing God's transforming power at work in us.

> *Search me, O God, and know my heart;*
> *test me and know my thoughts.*
> *See if there is any wicked way in me,*
> *and lead me in the way everlasting.*
> *(Ps. 139:23-24)*

Reflection

- What personal strengths do you bring to your mission work project? How can you build on them?

- What personal demons surface in you during times of stress? To what extent are your weaknesses simply your strengths taken to the extreme?

- What resources have helped you deal with your weaknesses— special prayers, scripture passages and other readings, or other spiritual disciplines?

Response

- Continue to practice your centering discipline, knowing it will be especially important for you under stress.

* List in your journal what you currently believe to be your personal strengths and weaknesses.

* Write yourself a message, rehearsing what you have learned about yourself and what you have learned about God that might help you during your mission project.

Prayer

Loving Creator God, thank you for the ways you are working in my life. Forgive my resistance and open my heart that I may indeed become more fully what you intend for me to be. In the name and love of Jesus. Amen.

And this is my prayer, that your love may overflow more and more with knowledge and full insight to help you to determine what is best, so that in the day of Christ you may be pure and blameless, having produced the harvest of righteousness that comes through Jesus Christ for the glory and praise of God. (Phil. 1:9-11)

Part Two

During Your Mission Project

Theme 1

Discovering God Already at Work

BIBLE STUDY

Reading: Isaiah 65:17-24

Commentary

The people to whom Isaiah articulated this vision were no doubt discouraged by the political, economic, and social problems facing them. "Where in the world is God?" they may well have cried. Isaiah's poetic and hopeful words assure us today that, regardless of our experience in the present moment, God is indeed at work among us. Peace, justice, and well-being for God's children are already in process. Micah (4:1-4), Jeremiah (31:31-34), and other prophets, while bemoaning the unfaithfulness of the people, also proclaimed God's intention to bring about a new and happy future. Jesus of Nazareth not only declared that the kingdom of God is at hand (Mark 1:15), but he also showed us how to live out and claim that promise.

David J. Lawson, in *Hungering for the Future*, summarizes the biblical conviction

They shall not labor in vain, or bear children for calamity; for they shall be offspring blessed by the Lord —and their descendants as well. Before they call I will answer, while they are yet speaking I will hear.
—*Isaiah 65:23-24*

that the battle has been won, that the powers of decay and destruction will be defeated, and that God's perfect rule of shalom can be expected. In spite of the many ways life on earth falls short of that vision, in spite of frustration, discouragement, and human tragedy, the perfect reign of God is at hand. The mission of the church is to serve as both its sign and its promise.[1]

Reflection on scripture

- What specific characteristics of "God's perfect rule of shalom" does Isaiah 65:17-24 mention?

- When and where do you see life on earth reflect this vision?

- What does it mean for you and your church to be the sign and the promise of God's perfect reign?

Reflection on your experience

- Recall what you learned from your reading about the natural resources and geography of your mission area. How has geography influenced its development and history?

- Where do you see the natural resources put to good use? What further potential do you see for their use?

- Recall from your reading the human decisions that have affected the course of history and current situation of this area. To what extent has God's will for justice been fulfilled? What injustices still exist?

- How does the church in this setting serve as the sign and the promise of God's perfect reign?

- How can you and your team serve as the sign and the promise of God's perfect reign?

Response

- Consider how your mission project aligns with what God wills for this place. What else can you do to help fulfill God's purposes here?
- Continue to practice your centering discipline regularly.

Prayer

Holy and eternal Creator, open my eyes so I may see how you are working in this place and in my heart that I may truly desire your will to be done. Strengthen my resolve to serve you and to participate in the coming of your kingdom. In Jesus' name. Amen.

He has told you, O mortal, what is good;
and what does the Lord require of you
but to do justice, and to love kindness,
and to walk humbly with your God?
(Mic. 6:8)

Theme 2

Experiencing Hospitality

BIBLE STUDY

Reading: Deuteronomy 10:17-19
Commentary

In Old Testament times, when no inns or public accommodations for travelers existed, many different tribes and nations considered hospitality to strangers a sacred obligation. Every home, every family, no matter how poor, was expected to provide food, shelter, and protection for travelers. Although inns did exist by New Testament times, Jews and early Christians opened their homes and guest quarters to others, as did Mary and Martha and the owner of the Upper Room to Jesus and his disciples.[2]

Jesus told parables illustrating both generous hospitality to those outside our usual social circles (Luke 14:12-14) and the importance of accepting hospitality freely offered to us (Matt. 22:1-10). Paul includes "hospitality to strangers" in his list of recommended behaviors for followers of Christ (Rom. 12:13), and the practice of hospitality is included among the good

You shall also love the stranger, for you were strangers in the land of Egypt.
—Deuteronomy 10:19

works commended by the writer of First Timothy (5:10). The Bible throughout presents hospitality not just as a gracious social act but as a true measure of one's obedience to God.

Reflection on scripture

* How does Deuteronomy 10:17-19 portray God?

* According to this passage, what does God expect of us?

* How do you think the Hebrew people felt when they were "strangers in the land of Egypt"?

Reflection on your experience

* How does it feel to be a stranger? What positive feelings do you have? What negative feelings do you experience?

* Record in your journal unique aspects of the hospitality you have received. What feelings have you experienced in response to this hospitality?

* What might make it difficult for your hosts to offer you hospitality?

* Reflect on opportunities you have had to extend hospitality. How satisfied are you with your generosity? What would you like to have done differently? What got in the way?

Response

* African custom requires one to receive that which is offered, allowing others the blessing of giving. Receive graciously while you are a guest. Express thanks without patronizing or putting down your hosts.

* On the other hand, be careful not to impose on your hosts by making thoughtless requests. Your hosts may quickly say, "No problem," even when they have to go to considerable trouble and expense to fulfill your wishes.

Prayer

Thank you, God, for the hospitality, thoughtfulness, and kindness of these new brothers and sisters in faith. Bless them for their generosity, and grant them the peace that comes from knowing they have pleased you. In the name of your son Jesus. Amen.

Every generous act of giving, with every perfect gift, is from above, coming down from the Father of lights, with whom there is no variation or shadow due to change. (James 1:17)

Theme 3

Making Adjustments

BIBLE STUDY

Reading: Philippians 4:6-9
Commentary

The theme of adjusting to different circumstances occurs frequently in biblical stories. The Hebrews, wandering through the wilderness after escaping from slavery in Egypt, complained openly about the conditions in which they found themselves (Exod. 16:2; 17:3). Ruth, however, made such a good adjustment to her husband's country, faith, and family that she chose to stay with her mother-in-law even after her husband's death (Ruth 1:16). Much of Hebrew scripture deals with the grief of the Hebrew people in exile. And throughout his many travels, Paul found spiritual strength to cope with many challenging circumstances (2 Cor. 6:4-10).

Confidence in God's sustaining power, coupled with a sense of adventure, can free us to savor different climates, foods, and customs. Thomas Moore urges us to overcome the fear and insecurity that drive our attempts to "homogenize the planet, to make every place comfortably

Do not worry about anything, but in everything by prayer and supplication with thanksgiving let your requests be made known to God. And the peace of God, which surpasses all understanding, will guard your hearts and your minds in Christ Jesus.
—Philippians 4:6-7

predictable and controllable." Advocating a more open attitude, he suggests that "a philosophy of enchantment might inspire us to travel without a defensive attitude and annoying judgments, and with real appreciation for the simple things that hold the spirit of a place."[3]

Sometimes, in fact, discomfort signifies the learning of something new. Many mission volunteers affirm that moving out of their "comfort zones" has allowed God to work in their lives in new ways. Teachable moments occur more often when we are uneasy because of a change in circumstances than when we are complacent and content.

Reflection on scripture

- What discomforts did Paul and other early Christian missionaries experience? (2 Cor. 6:4-10) How did they respond?

- When in your life have you known "the peace of God, which passes all understanding," in spite of difficult or uncomfortable circumstances?

- What things that "you have learned and received and heard and seen" in the teachings of Christ should you "keep on doing"?

Reflection on your experience

- What adjustments in your current situation cause you the most difficulty? Why?

- Can you imagine never having experienced the particular comfort or convenience you currently miss? If you never expected to have that comfort or convenience again, how would you adjust?

- What aspects of your current situation are "worthy of praise" and sources of enchantment?

- What might you learn from this new situation?

Response

* In addition to regular daily practice of the centering discipline you began before leaving home, use it whenever you feel homesick or overwhelmed by your current situation. Add the Serenity Prayer attributed to Reinhold Niebuhr and used in Twelve-Step groups: "God, grant me the serenity to accept the things I cannot change, the courage to change the things I can, and the wisdom to distinguish the one from the other."

* Choose one challenging aspect of your situation and take control of it in some way, real or symbolic.

* Ask another team member to listen compassionately while you express your longing and frustration. End your sharing by shifting your focus to affirmation for those aspects you find "worthy of praise." Pray together, thanking God for all the aspects of your situation you can affirm and also for the challenges to your growth. Ask that person to continue to hold you in prayer.

* Find a way to ease someone else's adjustment by listening compassionately and/or by sharing something you brought with you or acquired since your arrival. Pray with and for that person as above.

Prayer

Lord of my life and all life, help me to trust you even when I am frightened or uneasy. Forgive and heal my weakness. Renew my courage and free me from all that limits my ability to serve you in this place. In Jesus' name and for his sake. Amen.

Therefore, since it is by God's mercy that we are engaged in this ministry, we do not lose heart. (2 Cor. 4:1)

Theme 4

Liberating Time

BIBLE STUDY

Reading: Romans 12:1-2

Commentary

M. Robert Mulholland expanded on this passage from Paul's letter to the Romans in *The Upper Room Disciplines 1997*. Recalling Mary's response to the Annunciation, he encourages us likewise to practice "radical abandonment and availability." Surely Mary had other plans, yet she responded obediently to the astonishing announcement of her impending motherhood, "Here am I, the servant of the Lord; let it be with me according to your word" (Luke 1:38). Mulholland continues, "Our redemption is not maintained by activities we do to please God. Our redemption is actualized by the daily offering of our very being to God."[4]

One evening during her work project at an orphanage in Russia, Becky Denby wrote in her journal, "Today has been a very rough day emotionally. The paint did not arrive and may never come. We went to take a walk, Jenny and I, and we were

Do not be conformed to this world, but be transformed by the renewing of your minds, so that you may discern what is the will of God— what is good and acceptable and perfect.

—Romans 12:2

absolutely swarmed by the children, so much so that we went back to our room after only ten minutes. This evening during our team meeting, as we shared our frustration over not being able to paint, Brent pointed out that maybe our purpose wasn't to finish the work. He reminded us that Jesus was swarmed by crowds when he walked about, people just wanting to touch him, as the children here try to touch us. Brent noted that this place is like a leper colony in that few are willing to touch these children, but he pointed out that we can be the hands of Jesus here. We were stunned, speechless."

Later in the week Becky observed, "A dramatic change came over us when we began to understand our real purpose in being here. Peace and fulfillment enveloped us, and we went out to be with the children every spare minute, praying for Jesus to work through us to bring them joy. We were not there just to work on the room—the materials might never come. We were there to be with the children."

Reflection on scripture
* What does it mean for you to present yourself "as a living sacrifice, holy and acceptable to God" in the particular context of your work project?
* In what ways do you need to be "transformed by the renewing of your mind"?
* If the will of God is "what is good and acceptable and perfect," what would that be in your current situation?

Reflection on your experience
* How does what you are doing here differ from what you expected to be doing?
* How do attitudes toward time here differ from those at home?

- What effect do those differences have on your attitudes and relationships?

- How are you observing Sabbath time in this setting?

Response

- Without diminishing the importance of your mission work, try to release any preconceived measures of your success.

- If work is delayed, consider possible fruitful uses for this "gift of time." Spend it in conversation with others, for rest and reflection, in prayer and meditation, for experiencing nature, for journaling.

- Continue to practice your centering discipline, especially when you struggle with frustration or impatience. Make a breath prayer of Mary's words: breathing in "Here am I;" breathing out "a servant of the Lord."

- To experience fully the natural surroundings in which you find yourself, sit quietly and look about you. Absorb the sights, smells, sounds, textures, and tastes of this place. Reflect on Genesis 1:31: "God saw everything that [God] had made, and indeed, it was very good."

- Invite someone to walk with you to explore the area around your work or living site. Be sure to ask first about safety concerns. Ask a resident of your mission area to tell you about the plants and trees or about wildlife you might find.

Prayer

Loving Creator God, thank you for your gifts of time, for the rhythm of night and day, for those moments in which I proceed as planned and for those in which I encounter surprises. Help me to receive graciously delays and changes in plans, remaining open to new possibilities and to your guidance and will. Amen.

But, in accordance with his promise, we wait for new heavens and a new earth, where righteousness is at home. Therefore, beloved, while you are waiting for these things, strive to be found by him at peace, without spot or blemish; and regard the patience of our Lord as salvation. (2 Pet. 3:13-15)

Theme 5

Meeting Jesus

BIBLE STUDY

Reading: Acts 11:1-18

Commentary

This story presents Peter as a pioneer in moving Christianity out of the confines of Judaism. Cornelius of Caesarea was "an upright and God-fearing man,...well spoken of by the whole Jewish nation" (Acts 10:22). Having been born a Gentile, however, he had not been circumcised, a requirement at that time both for admittance to the inner sanctuary of the Jewish synagogue and for Christian baptism. An ultraconservative group of Christian leaders in Jerusalem criticized Peter for eating with Cornelius and his friends, persons they considered unclean according to the Jewish tradition in which they had been raised.[5] Peter told them of the heavenly vision he had experienced and of his subsequent realization that God had given these men the gift of the Holy Spirit (Acts 11:15-17). According to this story, Peter's words silenced the objections of his critics and opened the door to admit Gentiles into the Christian community.

> *"If then God gave them the same gift that he gave us when we believed in the Lord Jesus Christ, who was I that I could hinder God?"*
> —*Acts 11:17*

Acts 15 dramatizes a similar conflict that occurred when Paul and Barnabas returned to Jerusalem from Antioch. Before the apostles and elders of the church, Paul and Barnabas argued that Gentiles should be welcomed into the faith and not "troubled" by a demand for circumcision.[6] When Paul later narrates this encounter, he states his conviction that "a person is justified not by the works of the law but through faith in Jesus Christ" (Gal. 2:16). The author of Ephesians boldly proclaims that Christ "has made both groups into one and has broken down the dividing wall, that is, the hostility between us" (2:14).

Reflection on scripture

* Why were the church leaders upset with Peter? When and where do you see this reaction in the church today?

* Describe Peter's vision. What did the Holy Spirit tell him to do?

* What convinced Peter that to exclude these persons would be to "hinder God"?

Reflection on your experience

* What prejudices of yours are being challenged as you encounter new friends at your mission site?

* Where do such prejudices come from, and why do people allow them to rule their thinking?

* What does Peter's vision and his interpretation of it invite you to do?

* How are you experiencing the breaking down of the dividing wall between you and other persons?

Response

* Continue your centering discipline, especially when encountering new friends.

* If you are not in a culture that regards eye contact as disrespectful, look deeply into the eyes of persons you meet,

remembering Bishop Reeves's assertion that "in every human encounter with another person we may become aware of Jesus, and meet with him."[7] Especially when two people do not speak the same language, eye contact provides a moving and meaningful way to communicate.

* Instead of judging others, ask yourself how you would react if you had been born into similar circumstances.

* Respect your hosts and other workers at your mission site as full partners in this project. Ask for and follow, as much as possible, their advice and suggestions.

* If you have brought gifts to share, find subtle and personal ways to do so. Avoid grand presentations that appear to show off your wealth and position. One thoughtful approach is to ask your host church group to see that the neediest persons receive what you have brought.[8]

* Learn and use hand gestures and greetings indigenous to your mission area, such as the Argentine cheek-kiss or the graceful Asian bow with palms held together at chin level. In Zimbabwe we learned to express respectful greetings by gently clapping our hands and slightly bending a knee. We also learned a warm handshake, first clasping hands, then thumbs, then hands again.

* Carry paper and pencil and invite new friends to write their names for you, since it is often difficult to understand the spelling of names in a different language. Ask for addresses too, if you are willing to send postcards or letters when you return home; but don't make promises you cannot keep.

Prayer

Lord of life, forgive the prejudices I have allowed to rule my thoughts and actions. Help me embrace others as brothers and sisters in Christ and to affirm the ways you are at work in all our lives. In the name of Jesus, our brother. Amen.

Part Two

Then Peter began to speak to them: "I truly understand that God shows no partiality, but in every nation anyone who fears him and does what is right is acceptable to him." (Acts 10:34-35)

Theme 6

Building a Team

BIBLE STUDY

Reading: Colossians 3:12-17

Commentary

This letter affirms the Christians at Colossae as "chosen ones, holy and beloved," clearly defining such status as a responsibility, not a privilege. The life of their community, it notes, must bear witness to "the joy of Christian living."[9]

The author of Acts describes the powerful influence of followers of Christ: "Now the whole group of those who believed were of one heart and soul, and no one claimed private ownership of any possessions, but everything they owned was held in common" (Acts 4:32). Indeed, "day by day the Lord added to their number those who were being saved" (Acts 2:47). Surely it was not just their generosity and sharing that won converts but the spirit shining through their behavior and relationships.

The social virtues of compassion, kindness, humility, meekness, and patience listed in Colossians 3:12 reflect

Let the word of Christ dwell in you richly; teach and admonish one another in all wisdom; and with gratitude in your hearts sing psalms, hymns, and spiritual songs to God. And whatever you do, in word or deed, do everything in the name of the Lord Jesus, giving thanks to God the Father through him.
—Colossians 3:16-17

Christian love as described in 1 Corinthians 13:4-7. These virtues temper our tendency toward individualism, self-centeredness, and competition, making human harmony possible. Practiced joyfully, these virtues shape the nature of a community, enriching the life of its members and attracting others who might want to join. Furthermore, the direct instruction to "teach and admonish one another in all wisdom" (Col. 3:16) expresses the ideal "that all the members of the church should accept, each in his [or her] own measure, a share of responsibility for the spiritual welfare of all."[10]

Conflict inevitably creeps into personal relationships. Jesus acknowledged this reality when he taught, "If another member of the church sins against you, go and point out the fault when the two of you are alone. If the member listens to you, you have regained that one. But if you are not listened to, take one or two others along with you, so that every word may be confirmed by the evidence of two or three witnesses" (Matt. 18:15-16). The author of Ephesians later cautioned, "Be angry but do not sin; do not let the sun go down on your anger, and do not make room for the devil" (4:26-27). The writer also advocates "speaking the truth in love," which he claims "promotes the body's growth in building itself up in love" (4:15-16). Conflict or not, Paul's advice to "Encourage one another and build up each other" (1 Thess. 5:11) affirms both a basic human need and a key to building good relationships.

Reflection on scripture

- What specific behaviors reflect "compassion, kindness, humility, meekness, and patience"?

- How do these scripture passages suggest groups should deal with differences and conflicts?

- About what would Christians "teach and admonish one another"?

Reflection on your experience

🖙 To what extent do your team members seem bound "together in perfect harmony"? Do some individuals seem isolated or left out or antagonistic toward the others? How can you reach out to those persons and offer "the peace of Christ"?

🖙 How well is your team dealing with conflicts and differences? What underlying issues need discussion and prayer?

🖙 What behaviors strengthen relationships and bring out the best in your team members? What would you like to change?

🖙 To what extent do you express "thanks to God" in all you do?

Response

🖙 Continue your centering discipline, especially when you feel tension among your teammates.

🖙 Share honestly with your team leader what you are feeling about the group's relationships and any observations you have made about what is happening. Team leaders have been trained to deal with various stages of group life and to check in with individuals frequently, monitoring moods and needs. The more they know about what is really going on, the more effectively they can lead the team. Support your team leader by expressing empathy in difficult circumstances and asking how you can help.

🖙 Practice effective communication skills, "speaking the truth in love," by expressing your feelings nondefensively and giving reflective feedback to others. When you feel anger, hurt, or frustration, say so without attacking others, beginning with the words "I feel...." When someone else appears upset or unhappy, offer your support by noting kindly and nonjudgmentally, "You seem...." Beware of feeling you have to fix whatever is bothering someone else. Often just having the opportunity to vent and knowing they are understood frees people to accept and deal with problems.

- Use the same communication skills to express positive feelings. "I am so excited about what we accomplished today," or "You seem really pleased…" Sharing good feelings builds intimacy and makes it easier to deal with tensions when they occur. Discipline yourself to say something positive to each team member at least once a day.

- If you find yourself in conflict with someone, try to avoid getting into win/lose debates; instead seek to understand each other's position and needs, brainstorming possible solutions that can satisfy both of you. Unless you are skilled in this no-lose approach to conflict management, you may need to ask a third party to help you.

Prayer

Lord, bless your children gathered here, hoping to do your will and to serve others in your name. Unite us by your love and in your love, that we may uplift and bring out the best in each other. Empower us to work through differences and conflict so we may better understand and help one another. In the name of Jesus, who gave his life for all. Amen.

Put away from you all bitterness and wrath and anger and wrangling and slander, together with all malice, and be kind to one another, tenderhearted, forgiving one another, as God in Christ has forgiven you. (Eph. 4:31-32)

Theme 7

Singing the Lord's Song

BIBLE STUDY

Reading: Psalm 100

Commentary

This psalm consists of two short hymns: one a call to worship and the other a confident declaration of God's greatness and dependability. Hebrew worshipers approaching the Temple for a service of thanksgiving sang the first hymn (vv. 1-3) as a processional. A choir within the Temple sang the last two verses in response, inviting the worshipers to come inside the Temple courts. The Hebrew people seem to have come to the Temple, their established place for praise and prayer, with gladness and delight, leaving behind their cares and burdens.[11]

Not all the psalms express such unfettered joy, but even those that focus on human suffering and woe usually end on a note of praise and trust in God. Worship affirmed the Israelites' belief in God's involvement with every detail of human existence, rehearsing God's saving acts in the past and present, anticipating

Enter his gates with thanksgiving, and his courts with praise. Give thanks to him, bless his name For the Lord is good; his steadfast love endures forever, and his faithfulness to all generations.
—Psalm 100:4-5

93

triumph yet to come, and encouraging them toward right living and service.[12]

Worship experiences at your mission site may reflect the spirit of Psalm 100 more than those in which you usually participate. You may wonder why people with fewer material possessions, less elaborate church facilities, and more difficult lives in general sometimes worship with greater enthusiasm and conviction than those of us with relative wealth, beautiful church buildings, and plenty of support services to ease our way. Perhaps affluence lulls us into believing that science and technology will save us. Perhaps those who have to struggle to survive know more keenly their dependence on God. Living "closer to the edge," facing daily the fragile nature of human life and the inevitability of death, those who live in developing countries—or underdeveloped areas of our own —cannot take life and comfort for granted. Their celebrations of God's saving grace do not focus just on long-ago events but affirm their daily experiences of joy and peace in the midst of an uncertain existence. You also may experience anew your dependence on God, now that you are out of your comfort zone, away from your usual support systems and illusions of security.

Reflection on scripture
- What affirmations of God does this psalm express?
- What life experiences might inspire such affirmations?
- In what difficult life situations might such statements express hope for the future?

Reflection on your experience
- Think about the various worship experiences in which you have participated during your project so far. How have they been like what you are used to back home? How have they been different?
- What feelings can you identify as you recall these experiences?

🐾 What team traditions and rituals most effectively nurture your relationship with God and one another?

Response

🐾 Continue your centering discipline and consciously practice a prayerful approach to each part of your day.

🐾 Practice the Jesus prayer, also called "the prayer of the heart," taught by the early church as a way for believers to maintain constant communication with God. Its words are simple: "Lord Jesus Christ, Son of God, have mercy upon me, a sinner." According to theology professor Robert E. Webber, praying this prayer repeatedly until it becomes "an integral part of the human heart and consciousness...makes constant connection with the celebration of our salvation in worship and fortifies the believer as he or she faces the powers and principalities of this world."[13]

🐾 Experiment with *lectio divina*, a four-step Benedictine method for scripture reading and prayer described by Corinne Ware in *Discover Your Spiritual Type*. In the first step, *lectio*, readers or listeners use all their senses to perceive and imagine details related to the passage. For the second step, *meditatio*, the passage is read again, and participants are invited to use their intellect to reflect on its meaning and significance. During the third reading, *oratio*, participants are invited to respond prayerfully out of their feelings. The final reading, *contemplatio*, is followed by a period of silence, during which participants use their intuition to internalize what has been read.[14] This practice, described in greater detail in Ware's book, as well as in other spiritual guidebooks, lends itself well both to private prayer and journaling and to group sharing.

🐾 As you participate in worship with your mission site hosts, even if you do not know the language, try to perceive how the service celebrates God's saving grace experienced in their lives. Identify and celebrate personal experiences of that grace in your own life as well.

* Experiment with the following suggestion from Judy Wollen, volunteer-in-mission coordinator for Armenia and the Balkans. Sing along with fellow worshipers, even when you know neither the language, the lyrics, or the tune. Let the Spirit move you and sing whatever words come into your mind. Judy reports that this practice not only allows her to worship fully with brothers and sisters in Christ anywhere but also results in a flow of words that challenge and enlighten her.

* Savor the rituals that evolve for your team, symbolizing the meaning of your shared experiences and strengthening the bonds of your relationships.

Prayer

Eternal, all-powerful One, I praise you for your mighty acts, for the beauty of your creation, for your constant love. Even when your purposes are not clear to me, I bow in trust. Show me the way to serve you, and empower me with your spirit to live as your son Jesus taught, that others may know and do your will. Amen.

"The hour is coming, and is now here, when the true worshipers will worship the Father in spirit and truth, for the Father seeks such as these to worship him. God is spirit, and those who worship him must worship in spirit and truth." (John 4:23-24)

Theme 8

Maturing in Christ

BIBLE STUDY

Reading: Psalm 51:1-12

Commentary

This psalm serves as an appropriate prayer on a day when I am feeling out of sorts. Historically, however, it appears to have more consequential roots. Its heading in the Revised Standard Version —"A Psalm of David, when the prophet Nathan came to him, after he had gone in to Bathsheba"—suggests that this psalm, although probably not actually composed by David, was inspired by his repentant confession after that earlier incident. Expressing the agony of one alienated from God because of his or her own sin, the psalm does not blame other persons, as do some of the other lamenting psalms. It accepts guilt and seeks a cure—not just corrective action, but "a new and right spirit." The acknowledgment that animal sacrifice cannot accomplish what can be done only through repentance and a "broken and contrite heart" indicates that

Create in me a clean heart, O God, and put a new and right spirit within me. Do not cast me away from your presence, and do not take your holy spirit from me.
—Psalm 51:10-11

this psalm comes to us from a somewhat later period than the time of David's reign.[15]

Casting himself on God's mercy, the psalmist admits his failings, almost with relief that the secret is out. No longer must he hide and pretend. Verse 4 reflects a mature understanding that our offenses against others are indeed offenses against God. Although verse 5 seems to offer some sort of defense, perhaps even implicating God for making us as we are, verse 6 affirms God's desire for us. "Sin is therefore not God's choice for [us]; it is [our] choice for [ourselves]."[16] The psalmist declares that he needs more than forgiveness; he in fact needs "a clean heart" and "a new and right spirit." We can achieve neither by our own striving but only by opening ourselves to God's saving grace.

Saint John of the Cross in his classic work titled *Dark Night of the Soul* compares God's purging action on the soul to the action of fire upon a wooden log. All moisture and impurities must be driven out, causing ugliness and odor, before the log can become one with the fire. Likewise our imperfections must be consumed before we can abide in full unity with God, "enkindled in love."[17] Our transformation may be a painful process because we have so much imperfection to be transmuted. Yet God assures us, in the words of a hymn written two centuries ago:

> When through fiery trials thy pathways shall lie,
> my grace, all sufficient, shall be thy supply;
> the flame shall not hurt thee;
> I only design thy dross to consume
> and thy gold to refine.[18]

Reflection on scripture

- How would you define sin as used in this psalm?
- What does the psalmist fear most as a consequence of his or her sin?
- What does the psalmist ask God to do?

Reflection on your experience

* When in life are you most aware of your sin? What about during this mission project?

* Look back over the list of your strengths and weaknesses that you wrote in your journal before leaving home. To what extent are your strengths in play in your current situation? What help or encouragement do you need in order to employ those strengths?

* To what extent are your weaknesses surfacing? What might help you deal with them?

* What "new and right spirit" do you need God to give you?

Response

* Continue your centering discipline and practice of prayerful approaches to each part of your day.

* In your journal and—to whatever extent you feel comfortable—with your teammates, acknowledge the attitudes and behaviors that fall short of your best intentions. Since denial and covering up may take a great deal of energy, experience the release of confession and receive the assurance of absolution.

* Covenant with your teammates to support one another's personal growth through prayer, encouragement, mutual accountability, and positive reinforcement.

Prayer

Eternal, loving Creator God, you know me better than I know myself. You know my strengths, and you know my weaknesses. Help me surrender to your transforming power. Grant me patience and courage through the trials I must endure in order to be made perfect in your sight and in order to become a true instrument of your grace. In the name of Jesus, who faced his trials with grace and confidence in you. Amen.

He said to me, "My grace is sufficient for you, for power is made perfect in weakness." (2 Cor. 12:9)

Part Three

After Your Return

Theme 1

Discovering God Already at Work

Becky Denby returned from her work in a Russian orphanage, struggling with her sense of vocation. In her personal journal she expressed a longing "...*not* to work in an office anymore but to work as I did in Russia. But how? I am not trained to teach, nurse, do social work, or work in any field where I would interact with people in need. Shall I go back to school? Seek mission work? Or am I to be content here with kind words and deeds to those around me? I want to do like I did in Russia last summer. What do you want me to do, God?"

Moved by the shabby clothing worn by the orphanage children, and especially by their lack of socks, Becky spent the fall speaking to various groups about her experience. She and others from her team organized a drive to collect clothing to send back to Russia. "We spoke and spoke about those little feet in too large shoes with no socks. Shoes that rubbed up and down—the need for socks." They shared a list of other needed items: crayons,

I heard a loud voice from the throne saying, "See, the home of God is among mortals. He will dwell with them as their God; they will be his peoples, and God himself will be with them; he will wipe every tear from their eyes. Death will be no more; mourning and crying and pain will be no more, for the first things have passed away." And the one who was seated on the throne said, "See, I am making all things new."
—*Revelation 21:3-5*

coloring books, underwear, clothing. "Then the items seemed to multiply—not just one coloring book but bags full; not just a few boxes of crayons but hundreds; socks arrived in boxes and grocery bags full to overflowing....In the end, we collected and sent back to Russia forty-seven boxes and eight duffel bags filled with donated items."

In addition to providing ongoing support for mission projects where they have served, short-term mission volunteers often spur their churches to increased mission giving and more personal involvement in mission at home as well. In Lubeck, West Virginia, interest in local mission projects, quickened by the enthusiasm of a young man who served with a conference team in Russia in 1994, has been further stimulated since then by annual work-team projects closer to home. In July 1997, a team of twenty-five youth and adult leaders went to Washington, D. C., where they worked at three different inner-city mission sites. By arrangements made through The United Methodist General Board of Church and Society, some served meals to homeless persons; some worked with "gleaners" picking up surplus foods; others worked in a food bank.

Mindy came home determined to find out how people in her own town were already helping others and how she could pitch in. She shared her experiences with the Key Club (a service organization) and organized a local clothing drive, as well as a fund-raising dinner at her church to help send money to Washington for the work projects. Mindy also helped organize a canned-food drive at Halloween, collecting over two thousand canned food items for the local food pantry. The youth in her church help with a dinner for homeless persons four times a year and an annual Christmas dinner at which they package food donations and wrap gifts for a needy family. Recently they raised funds for a Habitat for Humanity House to be built in their community. One of them commented, "Going to work in the Washington mission centers helped us even more than we helped others. Being part of something that helps others helps me feel good about myself."

Volunteers who worked at the Princess Basma Center for Disabled Children in a Palestinian section of Jerusalem in 1998 gained a deepened understanding of the Arab-Israeli conflict there. They came home and wrote letters to the President of the United States to encourage his role in the peace process. After working in Argentina, team members resolved to learn more about the International Monetary Fund, the World Bank, and the impact of national debt on less industrialized nations. Increased understanding of the life of the poor might inspire mission volunteers to advocate for more humane legislation in such areas as health insurance for children, sweatshop and child-labor regulation, and welfare. An intensified appreciation for economic development programs enabling persons to develop independence and autonomy might prompt mission-project veterans to challenge their churches and communities to offer job readiness, training, and placement programs.

My most recent mission ventures have deepened my awareness of God's call to bring healing in the most difficult circumstances and in the face of obvious evil. In Argentina we walked with the Mothers of the Plaza de Mayo, who for twenty-three years have witnessed to the loss of their loved ones, "the disappeared." Although the military oppressors are no longer in power, many still have avoided accountability for the kidnappings, murders, and destruction of all records related to more than thirty thousand persons who disappeared during the 1970s. In Kosovo, I was inspired by courageous teachers, community leaders, and humanitarian workers struggling to restore some semblance of normalcy for refugees returning to ruined homes and villages. The United Methodist Committee on Relief focuses on housing reconstruction, food security (distributing tools and seeds and repairing farm equipment), and social development (reopening schools and forming parent-teacher councils), while other agencies work on demining, removing corpses from wells, and reestablishing water supply and basic sanitation. Mindful of similar atrocities occurring in Africa and elsewhere, we have to ask why the outpouring of aid for

Kosovo has not been matched in Sierra Leone and other troubled countries. Along with some other United Methodist bishops' spouses, I have covenanted to support UMCOR's relief and recovery efforts. We are committed to addressing the root causes of human selfishness, greed, prejudice, hatred, and cruelty wherever they occur. We know that counseling and mediation training are essential because traumatized children, if not helped to heal, may grow up to be terrorists themselves. We cannot afford to look the other way, to allow evil to reign because of our naïveté and ignorance.

A short-term mission volunteer, somewhat overwhelmed by her experience abroad and uncertain how to live with her new understanding of human need and God's call in her life, asked her team leader what she should do next. "Go home and love your country more," he responded gently. "Love your community more, love your church more, love your family more. God will show you new ways to serve."

Indeed, as Thomas Moore suggests in *The Re-Enchantment of Everyday Life*, "If we could really love the place where we were born and the place where we live, and let its history, geography, and genius enter our lives and affect them in every aspect, then we might not be so fearful when we meet people who love their place and its own ways, and more positively, we might find the security we need in the ground under our feet."[1]

Once Jesus was asked by the Pharisees when the kingdom of God was coming, and he answered, "The kingdom of God is not coming with things that can be observed; nor will they say, 'Look, here it is!' or 'There it is!' For, in fact, the kingdom of God is among you." (Luke 17:20-21)

Reflection

* What ongoing needs encountered at your mission project site can you address now that you have returned home?

* Consider the interplay of geography (location and natural resources) and politics (decisions and actions of individuals and groups) in your home community. With what special gifts has your community been blessed?

* What decisions by groups and individuals have brought suffering to your area? What actions have brought blessing? What do you think is God's will for those who live there?

* What forces currently work together for good? How can you align yourself with them? What forces work against God's will? How can you work to help overcome those forces?

* What service and economic development projects already underway in your church and community can you support? How?

Response

* Seek and gratefully receive opportunities to share the story of your experience and to enlist others in projects that will benefit the mission projects in which you have been involved.

* Invite persons you know to be seeking God's will for their lives to join you in considering the reflection questions above. Choose something you feel God wants you to do in your local community, and plan how you can mutually support one another in that venture. Find local organizations already working for and with the poor, and discover how you can support them. Consider participating in a Communities of Shalom program, described on page 161.

* Evaluate local, state, and national legislation by asking, "How will this impact the poor?" Lobby accordingly.

* Continue to practice your centering discipline, seeking God's guidance for both the large and small decisions of your life.

Prayer

Thank you, God, for giving me this place—this nation, this community, this home. Wrench the blinders from my eyes that I may see how you are working here. Open my ears that I may hear your call to work with you in realizing your vision of shalom. In the name of Jesus, who proclaimed the reality and presence of your kingdom. Amen.

Happy are those who consider the poor;
the Lord delivers them in the day of trouble.
(Ps. 41:1)

Theme 2

Experiencing Hospitality

AFTER HIS MISSION project experience, one volunteer began to rethink his attitude toward the friends his daughter brought home with her. Instead of feeling inconvenienced and annoyed by their arrival near dinnertime, he decided to welcome them and prepare a festive meal. Instead of judging their home life and lack of experience with family table manners, he engaged them in warm and friendly conversation.

Later, when his daughter brought these same friends to a church gathering, he noted the shocked reaction of other church members to their rowdy and boisterous behavior. He struggled with how to bridge this gap, how gently and lovingly to open the hearts of church members to those from different backgrounds, how gently and lovingly to guide the guests in learning expected behaviors without causing them to feel put down or criticized.

Participation in short-term mission projects has challenged my customary response to street beggars. I used to refuse them comfortably, content in the

Do not neglect to show hospitality to strangers, for by doing that some have entertained angels without knowing it.

—Hebrews 13:2

knowledge that I support soup kitchens and other programs through my church and convinced that giving handouts encourages dependency. Mission experiences have made me more aware of the humanity of street persons and eager to find effective ways to interact with them. Although I have not yet found a satisfactory solution for use in every situation, I can no longer walk by homeless persons or beggars as if I do not even see them. At the very least, I look them in the eye and smile a blessing. Sometimes I give cash or share snack food, if I am carrying any. Sometimes I have invited a street person into a restaurant and paid for a meal.

Recently my husband, while at Union Station in Washington, D.C., responded to the solicitation of a hungry middle-aged man by inviting him to sit down to eat with him. Over pizza and sodas, my husband learned the poignant story of the man's personal tragedies and descent into alcoholism. He also learned of a church that has taken the man into its fellowship, welcomes him to its services and coffee hour, and prays with him each day that he will be able to resist the urge to start drinking again.

It is too easy to dismiss others by drawing judgmental conclusions: "If they would just get a job," or "That would never happen to me." I was an adult myself before I realized that my own mother, divorced with three young children, would have had to choose between going on welfare or leaving us in day care so she could work, had it not been for the financial support of her father, who willingly took us all into his home. That knowledge drives me to my knees in gratitude and then to my feet again in service.

For you were called to freedom, brothers and sisters; only do not use your freedom as an opportunity for self-indulgence, but through love become slaves to one another. (Gal. 5:13)

Reflection

* What blessings have eased the difficulties of your life?

* How does Hebrews 13:2 invite you to change your practice of hospitality?

* What changes would you like to make in your own behavior or in the behavior of persons in your own home or church?

* How might you persuade others to participate in these changes?

Response

* Try to imagine how strangers might feel coming into your church. How could you put them at ease and make them feel welcome? Whom could you enlist to help make hospitality a priority in your church?

* Who are the strangers and outcasts in your community? What resources and support services are available? Volunteer to work in a soup kitchen, food pantry, or clothing thrift shop. Observe ways to preserve the dignity of those who need to use these services. Strike up conversations with individuals and learn their stories.

* Continue your centering discipline, focusing on gratitude for the blessings that have graced your life and seeking direction for ways to bless others.

Prayer

Father-Mother God, thank you for the way you have worked in my life, for the grace that has come through my family and my community to me, easing my way and providing both what I have needed and unlimited possibilities. Help me show my gratitude by sharing freely with others. Amen.

For the whole law is summed up in a single commandment, "You shall love your neighbor as yourself." (Gal. 5:14)

Theme 3

Making Adjustments

Wꜰ HENEVER I RETURN to our home from a short-term mission project, I exult in its spaciousness, cleanliness, and convenience. Sometimes I think guiltily that we could invite several other families to move in with us and still live more comfortably than most of the people in the world. Sadly, my renewed sense of mission and increased desire to serve God more faithfully often get buried in the reentry process as I sort mail, launder clothes, pay bills, and catch up on local news.

Once when we were describing our work-project experiences and the adjustments we have had to make while at a mission site, a young friend commented, only half jokingly, "My idea of an inconvenience is when I can't get good reception on my television set." *How true!* I thought. In the midst of our plenty, such trivial matters irritate and annoy us, well out of proportion to their importance.

Donella Meadows wrote an editorial column inspired by Peter Menzel's 1995 book *Material World: A Global Family Portrait.* Noting that the average American home boasts an area of more than two

Not that I am referring to being in need; for I have learned to be content with whatever I have. I know what it is to have little, and I know what it is to have plenty. In any and all circumstances I have learned the secret of being well-fed and of going hungry, of having plenty and of being in need. I can do all things through him who strengthens me.
—Philippians 4:11-13

thousand square feet, she reported the following living space for typical families in specific places: Shinka, Bhutan—726 square feet for thirteen people; Havanna, Cuba—1400 square feet for nine people; Kouakourou, Mali—990 square feet for eleven people; Ulan Bator, Mongolia—200 square feet for six people; Maïssade, Haiti—325 square feet for six people; Tel Aviv, Israel—667 square feet for four people; and Shiping, Yuhan, China—600 square feet for nine people. While we tend to measure our personal value by the size and luxuriousness of our homes, Donella concludes that most of the people in the world "are simply grateful to have shelter from the weather and a place to sleep in peace…to love their children, do their work, have fun, test and develop their souls, rejoice in life."[2]

While we were painting the fence at a rehabilitation center for disabled children in Jerusalem in January of 1998, Walter Griffith confided that he had never in his life been as content as he was the year he and his wife Jane spent at Red Bird Mission in Kentucky. "We had only the bare necessities," he noted, "no television, no daily newspaper—just the Sunday edition. When we go back home, we are such slaves to our stuff. We have to mow the lawn and take care of so many things. Working to help others feels so much better!" When I asked him how their life had changed because of this new awareness, he grinned, "We're getting rid of things. They just don't seem so important anymore."

Becky Denby noted in her journal nearly a year after her trip to Russia, "Things aren't as important to me anymore as are people and the time I spend with those I love. And my faith continues to grow and get stronger, firmer. It took a trip out of my comfort zone to a faraway land to put life in perspective for me."

Norma Denning mused, "Not a day goes by without my remembering our friends in Nicaragua. Every time I go in a grocery store and see all the things available to me, I think of how little they have; and I don't buy what I do not need. I'm mindful that there are needy children in our own community too and I'm looking for ways to reach out and share Christ's love with them."

Dr. Siang-Yang Tan and Dr. Douglas H. Gregg, in *Disciplines of the Holy Spirit*, encourage fasting as a way to invigorate our prayer life and deepen our relationship with God, to increase our self-discipline, and to strengthen us in the face of difficulties and temptations. They offer several suggestions for normal fasting but also propose fasting from media, human interaction, and especially from "our gluttonous consumer culture—our tendency to buy more and more things." Tan and Gregg conclude that fasting can be interpreted as any voluntary cessation of a usual activity for spiritual reasons, noting that "We surrender to God whenever we give up a regular activity in order to be more attentive to his presence and receptive to his will and purpose."[3]

"Fasting is a reminder that there are other values besides self-gratification and meeting our own needs," affirms Justo González in *When Christ Lives in Us*. He further explains that true renunciation is not about punishing ourselves by depriving ourselves of comforts or by suffering for the sake of suffering. "It is about traveling light on the road with Jesus. It is about leaving behind those things that will become a hindrance or that will be entirely inappropriate for the path we are taking."[4]

"Do not store up for yourselves treasures on earth, where moth and rust consume and where thieves break in and steal; but store up for yourselves treasures in heaven, where neither moth nor rust consumes and where thieves do not break in and steal. For where your treasure is, there your heart will be also." (Matt. 6:19-21)

Reflection

* Do you own your things, or do they own you? In what ways do you experience the "tyranny of possessions"?

- To what extent is your self-image caught up in what you have, instead of who you are?

- How could you simplify your lifestyle?

- What experience have you had with fasting?

Response

- Consider as a victory every decision not to buy something, every decision to get along without whatever is advertised or promoted, every decision to give away something you already own. Use this checklist for "Buy Nothing Day," observed annually in Seattle:

> Do I need it? How many do I already have?
> How long will it last?
> Could I borrow it from a friend or family member?
> Am I able [and willing] to clean, lubricate, and maintain it myself?...
> Will I be able to repair it?
> Have I researched it to get the best quality
>   for the best price?
> How will I dispose of it when I'm done using it?
> Are the resources that went into it renewable
>   or nonrenewable?
> Is it made of recycled materials and is it recyclable?
> Is there anything that I already own that I could
>   substitute for it?"[5]

- Read or talk with someone about fasting. Experiment with simple fasts either from food or some other activity, during which times you intentionally find ways to draw closer to God. Bear in mind Jesus' admonition in Matthew 6:16: "And whenever you fast, do not look dismal, like the hypocrites, for they disfigure their faces so as to show others that they are fasting. Truly I tell you, they have received their reward."

- Study, by yourself or with a small group, the life and teachings of Saint Francis of Assisi, who turned his back on his family's wealth and embraced poverty in order to serve Christ and humankind.

- Either by yourself or with a small group, study a resource book such as *'Tis a Gift to Be Simple: Embracing the Freedom of Living with Less,* by Barbara DeGrote-Sorensen and David Allen Sorensen, or *Living Simply,* by Delia Halverson. See Resources, page 160, for more information about these books.

- Participate in a group study using the resource *Curing Affluenza,* a six-session study available through EcuFilm. See Resources, page 160, for details on how to order.

- As you simplify your lifestyle, find ways to channel what you save into mission.

- Continue to practice your centering discipline at least daily, and especially when you feel caught up by desire for unnecessary things.

Prayer

Holy Creator and Sustainer of Life, you have given me all I need and more. Forgive my greed and obsession with material things. So fill me with your love that following your commands becomes more important than my comfort and possessions. Keep me mindful of those truly in need so that I may share your abundance according to your will. In the name of Jesus, who lived and loved freely. Amen.

Do not love the world or the things in the world. The love of the Father is not in those who love the world; for all that is in the world—the desire of the flesh, the desire of the eyes, the pride in riches—comes not from the Father but from the world. And the world and its desire are passing away, but those who do the will of God live forever. (1 John 2:15-17)

Theme 4

Liberating Time

I ALWAYS FEEL SOMEWHAT defensive of Martha when I hear the story in Luke 10:38-42. She must have felt rebuked by Jesus, and she must have resented Mary's choice to sit at his feet, listening to him rather than helping with preparations for their guests. I'm sure Martha wanted to listen to Jesus too, but if she was like me, she probably felt driven to get the work done first—and to unnecessarily high standards. I have had to learn the hard way that sometimes a can of soup opened with love and joy is more appreciated than an elegant meal and elaborate table setting prepared by an exhausted hostess.

Dr. John Claypool, during a 1988 lecture series for pastors in Ohio, suggested that perhaps one reason the Samaritan stopped to help the injured man on the Jericho road was that he was not under as much pressure as were the priest and the Levite. Perhaps he did not have to "worry about getting to his next appointment on time or leaving myriad tasks undone."[6] When we schedule ourselves too tightly, we do not leave room for the unexpected, for the stranger in

Now as they went on their way, he entered a certain village, where a woman named Martha welcomed him into her home. She had a sister named Mary, who sat at the Lord's feet and listened to what he was saying. But Martha was distracted by her many tasks; so she came to him and asked, "Lord, do you not care that my sister has left me to do all the work by myself? Tell her then to help me." But the Lord answered her, "Martha, Martha, you are worried and distracted by many things; there is need of only one thing. Mary has chosen the better part, which will not be taken away from her."

—Luke 10:38-42

need, or even for a loved one's request. Although I often resolve to live every moment for God, my idolatrous and workaholic love of accomplishment can drive me to be so caught up in my own busy-ness that I cannot respond to an unexpected opportunity. I might not even notice it!

I seem to be possessed by a mind that can dream up more things to do than I have time for, as well as numerous details to complicate my projects. Probably on my deathbed I will utter my usual lament for the end of time allotted to a task: "I could have used one more day." Would I perhaps be a more effective instrument of God's grace if I left time for the unexpected, opening myself for God's gift of service opportunities that I have not planned on, rather than trying to cram as much accomplishment as possible into a day? What if I were to schedule tasks for only some of the time available, leaving the rest for whatever opportunities arise? What if I were to stop working on whatever project engages me before time runs out, rather than racing to get more done. Might I then possibly be more readily responsive to the needs of others? However deeply motivated our personal ministries may be, if they result in a tyranny of agendas that prohibits us from loving deeds and acts of kindness, if they leave us breathless and ragged and resentful, then perhaps we need to reorder our priorities.

Norma Wimberly, during a stewardship workshop at a Transformation 2000 event in the fall of 1997, declared, "Time is our most precious resource. There is never enough time to do all the things we want to do, but we all have the same twenty-four hours a day. We have to set priorities, and sometimes that means we have to simplify. When I put God first, I have all the time I need. I have to learn to manage myself in the time I've been given. Living out the principle of the tithe means that I must constantly ask myself, 'What is the next thing that God wants me to do, in spite of what my list says? What do I need to do tomorrow to serve God, to feel productive, to take care of me?'"

If we do not take care of ourselves—physically, emotionally, and spiritually, we have less to give those who depend upon us. Perhaps that is why the early Hebrew people honored the observance of Sabbath time. Perhaps that is why we need so desperately to reestablish the priority of regular holy and healing times in our schedules.

> *Have you not known? Have you not heard?*
> *The Lord is the everlasting God,*
> *the Creator of the ends of the earth.*
> *He does not faint or grow weary;*
> *his understanding is unsearchable.*
> *He gives power to the faint,*
> *and strengthens the powerless.*
> *Even youths will faint and be weary,*
> *and the young will fall exhausted;*
> *but those who wait for the Lord shall renew their strength,*
> *they shall mount up with wings like eagles,*
> *they shall run and not be weary,*
> *they shall walk and not faint.*
> *(Isa. 40:28-31)*

Reflection

* Do you tend to be more like Mary or Martha?

* Look back at the list of priorities you recorded before your mission trip. How have they changed?

* Scott and Helen Nearing, New England pioneers in the "back to the land" movement of recent decades and authors of *The Good Life*, divided their daily activities into three four-hour blocks for physical work, professional activity, and civic responsibilities.[7] Make a pie chart illustrating how you spend your days. How consistently does the way you spend your time reflect the priorities you have listed?

- On what kinds of activities would you like to spend more time? On what would you like to spend less? How could you make those changes?

- What activities interfere most with what you really believe God wants you to do? How could you reduce or even eliminate the time you spend on them? What would you have to let go of to be more available to do God's will?

- What attitudes, beliefs, or fears motivate your busy-ness? Are you driven by an underlying conviction that by trying harder you can somehow ensure your own happiness and safety? What do the scriptures say to this? (Eccles. 9:11: "Again I saw that under the sun the race is not to the swift, nor the battle to the strong, nor bread to the wise, nor riches to the intelligent, nor favor to the skillful; but time and chance happen to them all.") Or do you believe you need to earn the love of God and of those most important to you? (Eph. 1:5-8: "He destined us for adoption as his children through Jesus Christ, according to the good pleasure of his will, to the praise of his glorious grace that he freely bestowed on us in the Beloved. In him we have redemption through his blood, the forgiveness of our trespasses, according to the riches of his grace that he lavished on us.")

Response

- Continue to practice your centering discipline at least once a day, especially when you feel pressured or stressed by time. Ask yourself, "What is it that God wants me to be doing right now?"

- Try a new approach to planning. Set aside blocks of time for the things you feel are most important. Include time for Sabbathing, for self-care, for spiritual and physical disciplines to strengthen soul and body, and for relationships. When you make a list of "things to do," anticipate that things often take longer than expected. Star those items that are "musts" and do them first; then if you run out of time, you can relax, knowing the other items can wait. Leave time for the unexpected. If activities are completed sooner than anticipated, consider that a gift of time.

- Receive as gifts of time those unplanned-for moments, such as waiting in line or at a stoplight, delays in your schedule or appointments, or even sleepless nights. Use such moments for prayer and meditation, for conversation, for reading, or for working on a project that interests you.

- Find a friend or small group with whom you can explore the underlying attitudes and beliefs that motivate your busyness. Covenant together to practice specific disciplines, such as those above, that will liberate you from drivenness and open you to new possibilities of freedom. Pray together for healing and wholeness.

Prayer

Creator God, forgive my preoccupation with deadlines and lists of things to do. Open my eyes and my heart, that gratitude for all your love has made possible in my life may overflow and touch those around me, my neighbors near and far. Amen.

For by grace you have been saved through faith, and this is not your own doing; it is the gift of God—not the result of works, so that no one may boast. (Eph. 2:8-9)

Theme 5

Meeting Jesus

NORMA DENNING fell in love with the children of Sandino City near the Nicaraguan capital of Managua, while working with a West Virginia team there in 1993, constructing a small Moravian church. While she did her share of brick and mortar work, Norma also made a special effort to spend time with the children who buzzed around the work site. "When I came home, I decided I had to act on my promise to provide Christmas presents for the children. I collected donations and sent them to the Managua Moravian Church for the purchase of the gifts." Each year since, Norma has collected more than $1,000, which the Managua church uses to buy clothing, food, and gifts for less fortunate families in the area of the Sandino City Church.

Becky Peters, after her first visit to Africa University in 1997, "adopted" two students on the verge of having to leave school for lack of funds to pay their fees. In addition to contracting with the university bursar to pay their bills, upon returning to her home she purchased and sent back to Africa University ten

There is no longer Jew or Greek, there is no longer slave or free, there is no longer male and female; for all of you are one in Christ Jesus.
—Galatians 3:28

keyboards for music instruction and several other items needed by particular students. She also has taken into her home for the holidays several African students attending colleges in the United States. Harry and Donna Light, who included in their family Christmas celebrations a Liberian theology student studying in Michigan, have crafted more than 250 wooden plaques to sell in order to raise funds for an Africa University scholarship. Team members have sent back money and gifts, sometimes by way of other teams going to the same location. Of particular concern have been the young children in the "Baby-fold" orphanage at Old Mutare Mission, across the road from Africa University. Later teams report that the children now have more diapers and clothing and other amenities, thanks to the continued involvement of and gifts from our volunteers. Becky Peters speaks for many other mission volunteers when she says, "I don't want any credit for what I do, as I know it is really God working through me. All the money I earn is His for me to use as He leads me."

Such ongoing relationships with and active support of new friends made during mission work projects may continue long after return from the mission site, but this only reflects part of the change that may take place in how volunteers relate to others. Months after her return, Becky Denby reflected, "I think for now my call is to perform simple acts of caring and kindness. Each day I realize more than ever that I am Christ's ambassador every second of the day and that my actions represent Christ to all the people I meet—or should. The memories I carry back from Russia of my time with the children there—a simple high-five, my hands outstretched with lotion for them to touch and smell, walking together holding hands, having a picture taken together—remind me to take more time to share with those with whom I come in contact here."

Yet on even a deeper level, volunteers who have truly entered into the life of a different place may understand more fully the impact of racism and white privilege and of economic inequities on persons' lives. Bishop Leontine J. C. Kelly described an encounter with a college student in Bolivia. Pointing to the tin miners now out of work because the United States of America was stockpiling tin, the student remarked, "We may be poor, but we are not stupid. We understand the relationship between your wealth and our poverty." Bishop Kelly also noted that in contrast to our expectation that working hard will result in our "getting ahead," people in other parts of the world struggle just to stay alive.

The power of systems and institutions, often associated with subtle and unrecognized prejudice, maintains white privilege throughout our world today. Indeed having the wherewithal and the freedom to participate in short-term mission projects is largely a white privilege, as are the freedoms to choose where we will reside and to live without the fear of unjust arrest, discrimination, and harassment. Thomasina Stewart describes the almost overwhelming sense of belonging she felt in Africa, as if she had indeed come home. "It was comforting to see lots of folks who looked like me," she said, "which doesn't happen much in West Virginia. It made me wonder about my ancestors. The void of information about the seventeen generations that links me to Africa tugged at my being. When a student asked me about relationships between blacks and whites in America today, I had to say that although things seem to have improved some, black folks still have to be cautious. You learn to expect unpleasant encounters and have to be prepared to handle them. When you discover people who do not have good intentions, you have to decide whether to take on that battle or walk away."

Audrey Stanton, a journalism major, signed up for a ten-day trip to Zimbabwe right after her college graduation. There she bonded with Africa University students and so enjoyed her experience that she volunteered to return for two months in the fall to help out in the public relations office. "Agriculture students gave me an understanding of how Africa University will help the continent harvest more efficiently to feed its millions. Students in the department of theology gave me a cross-cultural view of God. Business students demonstrated a passion to use their training to help support their families in faraway nations. And education students revealed to me an intense desire to learn, not for themselves, but so they can help their homelands by returning as teachers and community leaders. You will find students like these at any institution, but chances are they didn't walk for ten months across the continent to get to their school. Chances are they didn't leave hungry brothers and sisters back home in mud-floor huts to go learn something that could help their families in the long run. Chances are they didn't have to sacrifice everything they have to pay a $3,000 per year tuition."

"I always thought of myself as open-minded," Audrey continued, "but now I don't take anything for granted. When someone does something I don't understand, I realize that there must be a reason. On the other hand, I used to ignore racist jokes and remarks, but now when I hear them, I speak out and say, 'That offends me!'" Audrey, currently employed by a local newspaper, accepts invitations to speak to public school classes, anticipating these and other opportunities for correcting misinformed stereotypes of African people.

Karen David, upon return from work among Bosnian refugees with an Oklahoma mission volunteer team, asserted, "I came home more aware than ever that the world is really a small neighborhood. I was more convinced than ever that, if I am a Christian, my neighbors are not just the people next door or down the street. People all over the world are my neighbors, and we have much more in common than I ever knew."[8]

You do well if you really fulfill the royal law according to the scripture, "You shall love your neighbor as yourself." But if you show partiality, you commit sin and are convicted by the law as transgressors. (James 2:8-9)

Reflection

 How do Galatians 3:28 and James 2:8-9 challenge our perceptions of cultural differences?

 As you remember your new friends in Christ, think of the conditions that shape their lives. In what ways can you help fulfill God's purpose for them? Can you send gifts or provide continuing support for individuals or for mission projects? Is there relevant legislation for which you can lobby?

 Think about the people you encounter through your work and in your community. How can you learn more about their life circumstances and needs?

 How are you hurt by or how do you benefit from institutional racism and white privilege? What benefits are you willing to give up in order to provide more equal opportunity for others?

Response

 Remember your new friends by name in your prayers. Post their pictures as reminders of your shared experiences and of what you have learned through knowing them.

 Find ways to support them, either individually or through mission projects. Tell their stories and invite others to give gifts or make donations.

 Take time to get to know someone in your community whose experiences differ from your own.

 Practice meeting the eyes of others, acknowledging their sacred worth, even if you know nothing about them or if you find them difficult to understand. Pray for them, affirming God's work in their lives, even if you cannot see clear evidence of it.

 Read about institutional racism and white privilege. Look for examples in those organizations to which you belong. Speak up for inclusion and find ways to overcome barriers between groups of people. *First We Must Listen: Living in a*

Multicultural Society (Resources, 159) provides excellent material on this topic.

❧ Continue your centering discipline, especially when with others who need your attention and care.

Prayer

Father-Mother God, forgive my tendency to think more highly of myself than I ought to think and to consider myself deserving of more than my share of your blessings. Help me recognize my kinship to all your children, and free me to embrace them and to share with them your bounty. In the name of Jesus, who offered his life that all might be one. Amen.

What good is it, my brothers and sisters, if you say you have faith but do not have works? Can faith save you? If a brother or sister is naked and lacks daily food, and one of you says to them, "Go in peace; keep warm and eat your fill," and yet you do not supply their bodily needs, what is the good of that? So faith by itself, if it has no works, is dead. (James 2:14-17)

Theme 6

Building a Team

Mission volunteers returning from an intense group experience suddenly may feel cast adrift if no one else in their home church or community participated with them. Filled with enthusiasm and eager to share their adventures, they may be disappointed to find others expressing only mild interest in their stories. Family and friends, neighbors and colleagues may be somewhat puzzled or even put off by the volunteers' efforts to share details and feelings. Continuing contact with at least some members of the team, especially opportunities to share photographs and savor memories, can ease reentry and help participants process their changed perceptions and priorities.

Follow-up projects will sometimes elicit strong support and eager cooperation. Becky Denby, overwhelmed by the response to requests for shoes and clothing for the Russian orphanage children, described this experience in her journal: "One night in Disciple Class we shared our problem—too much stuff to carry. And presto, someone knew about a shipping company nearby. A price was

I therefore, the prisoner in the Lord, beg you to lead a life worthy of the calling to which you have been called, with all humility and gentleness, with patience, bearing with one another in love, making every effort to maintain the unity of the Spirit in the bond of peace. There is one body and one Spirit, just as you were called to the one hope of your calling, one Lord, one faith, one baptism, one God and Father of all, who is above all and through all and in all. But each of us was given grace according to the measure of Christ's gift.
—Ephesians 4:1-7

131

secured and cash was solicited to cover shipping costs, airfare for two persons to travel over to get the items through customs, and donations to our contacts in Russia and to the orphanage. We collected 4,700 pounds of items and raised thousands of dollars. We found a donor for the boxes and began to pack around the clock, weighing and binding under the direction of another volunteer with expertise in such matters. People brought in meals so we wouldn't have to cook."

Becky marveled, "The how-to of this project was never, ever planned nor was it thought through. What happened I believe was meant to happen. God used me to organize but also so many others who gave time, money, items. Without everyone helping, this could not have happened, but, oh, how the pieces fell into place. The day the truck pulled out from our church parking lot to take the forty-seven boxes and eight duffel bags to the plane was a result of teamwork. Our two representatives who traveled with the donations, a Russian contact person, and someone from the orphanage had to fight with customs officials for several days; but finally, thanks to our carefully itemized list of the contents of each container and master list totaling everything, the items went to the orphanage without any further fees being charged."

Richard Work started his project with a simple goal: to encourage his six-hundred-member church in Charleston, West Virginia, to fill twenty-five North Korea famine relief boxes. One family in the congregation, however, challenged him to think bigger by purchasing a large supply of cardboard boxes. "If you have the boxes, people will fill them," they explained. In the end, 835 boxes were filled by individuals, groups, and churches across the West Virginia Conference and shipped to North Korea through The United Methodist Committee on Relief (UMCOR). Richard points out that eighty-five percent of the congregations in West Virginia have two hundred members or less. Those small congregations were the most actively involved in this project. One church of about forty members sent a check for $500. "They responded to the call to be Christ-like by feeding the hungry," Richard declared. "How they felt about North Korea as a country had nothing to do with it."

Perhaps it takes concrete and dramatic challenges such as these to move people out of their normal routines. More often, we struggle with the tendency in our local churches for the same persons to do all the work. Sometimes it's easier just to ask the same ones rather than risk disappointment, but in so doing we deny others the opportunity to become part of the family.

Marsha Geiger described her church's housing rehabilitation projects as "the best quality sharing we've ever had. We get referrals through a local agency for people who need windows replaced or roofs or front porches repaired. We gather a team to work on a Friday and Saturday, including some with carpentry skills and others to provide meals, to go after needed supplies, or to provide child care. Once we painted a little church in a nearby community and saw it come alive and grow because of renewed interest sparked by the fresh coat of paint. People pulling together like that and seeing the results of their labor build relationships you can't get any other way!"

During team worship one evening in Zimbabwe, Joe Shreve read John 13:3-5, which tells about Jesus washing the feet of his disciples. Putting into words what we already felt in our hearts, Joe stated that "in serving we become family" and that sharing in even the humblest tasks makes us feel like we belong. Both by modeling mutual service and by providing opportunities for others to participate, we build up the body of Christ and strengthen our connections to one another.

Let the same mind be in you that was in Christ Jesus,
who, though he was in the form of God,
   did not regard equality with God
   as something to be exploited,
but emptied himself,
   taking the form of a slave,
   being born in human likeness.

And being found in human form,
   he humbled himself
   and became obedient to the point of death—
   even death on a cross.
   (Phil. 2:5-8)

Reflection

- In the various groups of which you are a part—family, church, work colleagues, neighbors—how can you more effectively model servanthood and mutual care?

- Who in those groups need affirmation of the gifts they bring to the whole, of the importance of their roles and responsibilities?

- What traditions and rituals in those groups affirm their particular missions and help to create a nurturing bond among the members?

Response

- If you have not already done so, invite your family, your church, your colleagues at work—or another group of which you are a part—to write a mission statement. This need not be complex but may simply state what you are about, what you hope to accomplish together.

- Discuss with other members of these groups what traditions and rituals are working well for you now, which you might like to change, and what you might like to add.

- Find ways to affirm members of those groups who may feel inferior or less valued than the others: the child who is at odds with the rest of the family, the custodian at church or at work, or the new member of a staff or organization.

- Learn more about effective communication skills and conflict management strategies. See Resources, pages 160–61, for information and suggestions.

- If you are not already part of a covenant prayer group, talk to your pastor and others who might be interested in starting one. See Resources, pages 161–62, for covenant group guidelines.

- Continue your centering discipline, particularly as you reenter and relate to groups of which you are a part.

Prayer

Loving God, I thank you for my family and other groups in which I experience loving, growing relationships. I know your presence in those relationships, guiding and healing and drawing us closer to you. Continue that good work in us, that together we may serve you in the world. In the name of Jesus, who calls us to follow his teachings and example. Amen.

"I ask not only on behalf of these, but also on behalf of those who will believe in me through their word, that they may all be one. As you, Father, are in me and I am in you, may they also be in us, so that the world may believe that you have sent me. The glory that you have given me I have given them, so that they may be one, as we are one, I in them and you in me, that they may become completely one, so that the world may know that you have sent me and have loved them even as you have loved me." (John 17:20-23)

Theme 7

Singing the Lord's Song

MISSION VOLUNTEERS returning home may long for the fervor and excitement of indigenous worship experienced at their mission site. During a service in Zimbabwe, we marveled at the enthusiasm with which each class meeting group danced and sang its way down the aisle to present a welcoming gift to their new pastor. Our team took a turn too, quickly putting together cash to present and singing a simple African chant we had learned. When the United Methodist Women's turn was announced, Clara Belle got up to join them, exclaiming, "I'm a United Methodist Woman too." The chairperson of the pastor-parish relations committee, a stately woman dressed in red, accompanied each group, blowing on a whistle as she twisted and swayed to the music. African celebrations often include whistle-blowing, we were told; hence its use in worship seems normal and natural. Sadly, we acknowledged that whistle-blowing, not to mention the lively dancing, would be unwelcome in most of the churches we know. We did participate once in an annual conference session

When the day of Pentecost had come, they were all together in one place. And suddenly from heaven there came a sound like the rush of a violent wind, and it filled the entire house where they were sitting. Divided tongues, as of fire, appeared among them, and a tongue rested on each of them. All of them were filled with the Holy Spirit and began to speak in other languages, as the Spirit gave them ability.
—Acts 2:1-4

during which worshipers were invited to dance their way forward African-style to present their offerings. Those present seemed to "get into it" for this occasion, at least, but that jubilant practice never replaced our more traditional practice of passing the offering plate.

As we try to describe the spiritual power present in indigenous worship, we may sense responses ranging from curiosity and amusement to outright fear that we might try to recreate such experiences back home. A wise team leader cautioned his volunteers, "Don't try to take your mother's church away from her." We may be able to conduct small experiments, an African chant here, the use of Russian icons or a Native American ritual there; but if we belittle the worship style and cherished traditions of our home churches, we only increase defensiveness and resistance to change.

Although some early missionary movements suppressed the use of native music and instruments in worship, the church coming of age all over the world has experienced a cultural revival, affirming that there are many ways to "sing the Lord's song." Raquel Mora Martínez, editor of *Mil Voces para Celebrar*, the new United Methodist Spanish language hymnal, credits some of this shift to the Second Vatican Council, called by Pope John XXIII. The Roman Catholic Church's decision to allow people to worship in their own language, along with a movement toward solidarity with the poor and oppressed, opened the door to a renewal movement still in process. Inclusive worship that incorporates and affirms the heritage of various cultures reflects a growing understanding that God is not "out there" somewhere but very present in human experience. Raquel suggests that perhaps the best way to help people appreciate the power of indigenous worship is to assist them in understanding their own culture first, in discovering how history and tradition have shaped their practices today. Then they may be more ready to experience other cultures and practices with an open mind and heart.

Meanwhile, however, for the many who do not feel at home

in our churches, we must offer multiple options. It is not enough for churches located in predominantly ethnic communities to offer indigenous worship. Ethnic persons have migrated out of cultural pockets into the mainstream of our cities and towns. In addition, the rapidly changing attitudes and values of each new generation create a need for appropriate and meaningful worship in communities that may still be offering only a limited menu of spiritual nurture. Church-growth consultants Bill Easum and Thomas Bandy, in *Growing Spiritual Redwoods*, maintain that "the gospel must be communicated in the language, cultural forms, and technology of the people you are trying to reach." Worship must accommodate differences in attitudes, preferences, and needs, not necessarily linked to such obvious characteristics as age or economic status. The traditional church service, for example, with its strict attention to form and its appeal to intellectual understanding, cannot satisfy the yearning of those who hunger for worship that "aims at the heart, rather than at the mind."[9]

In response to a growing awareness that people bring different needs to worship, Corinne Ware has developed an analysis of spiritual style, based on the work of Urban T. Holmes. In *Discover Your Spiritual Type*, she discusses four different approaches: 1) an intellectual, thinking style that responds to the spoken or written word and to order; 2) a heart-centered style that responds to emotional appeal and spontaneity; 3) a mystic style that focuses on the inner life; and 4) a visionary style with passion for transforming society. Ware provides assessment tools for individuals and congregations and proposes strategies both for more effectively meeting current needs and for nurturing growth. Ware challenges congregations to validate the individual spirituality of its members, while enriching its life by offering a more inclusive ministry "stretching toward some variety of expression without losing the central identity of the group."[10]

Returning mission volunteers may also find it difficult to maintain the intense level of personal communication with

God experienced during their project. Surrounded by the comforts of home, we may be less in touch with our dependence on God. All the more reason, then, to remind ourselves daily of the peace and joy we have found through frequent participation in prayer and other spiritual disciplines. It's important to start simply and not to be too hard on ourselves when we backslide. Art objects from our mission site, continued supportive relationships with other team members, and steadfast practice of those disciplines we have found most meaningful can help us maintain a close relationship with God.

Sarah Ban Breathnach, in *Simple Abundance*, her popular work on incorporating spirituality into our daily lives, borrows from Julia Cameron the image of God's power as a sort of spiritual electricity, available to us for the asking.[11] Prayer then is not just a listing of those matters about which we feel God should be taking some action but an act of connecting to the Source. By completing this connection, we can receive and serve as channels for spiritual energy that can transform both our own lives and that of our human community. To pray without ceasing is to receive spiritual power constantly and transmit it to others. Because most of us need considerable help maintaining a high level of spiritual functioning, we rely on our faith communities to keep us focused. Regular participation in the corporate worship of a congregation and in small covenant prayer groups sustains our spiritual connection and helps us resist the negative energies so prevalent in our world.

Dr. Siang-Yang Tan and Dr. Douglas H. Gregg list three categories of spiritual disciplines: "the disciplines of solitude (solitude and silence, listening and guidance, prayer and intercession, study and meditation), the disciplines of surrender (repentance and confession, yielding and submission, fasting, and worship), and the disciplines of service (fellowship, simplicity, service, and witness)." Through these disciplines, we can "receive from the Holy Spirit the power to do what we cannot do on our own: love our enemies, live without unnecessary worry, and give generously of our resources."[12] By drawing nearer to God in love and intimacy, we may not only find greater fulfillment in our personal lives but also minister more effectively in a broken world.

The fruit of the Spirit is love, joy, peace, patience, kindness, generosity, faithfulness, gentleness, and self-control. (Gal. 5:22-23)

Reflection

* Recall meaningful worship services in which you have participated. What have these experiences had in common? How have they differed from one another?

* What do the common elements of these meaningful worship memories tell you about your spiritual style?

* How have your worship needs changed over time and in response to changes taking place in your life?

* To what extent does the worship life of your church satisfy you? How do you think others in your church feel?

* When have you felt closest to God in your private, spiritual disciplines?

* What gets in the way of that closeness now?

Response

* Continue practicing your centering discipline and try to approach each part of your day with appropriate prayer.

* List in your journal the various disciplines (journaling, breath prayers, fasting, meditation, contemplation, *lectio divina*, solitude, intercessory prayer, listening, confession, praise) that you have tried, noting how effective and meaningful you found them. While currently some may seem more helpful to you than others, under different circumstances you may want to try the others again later.

* Take the self-test in *Discover Your Spiritual Type*. Do the results fit your self-perception? What new personal insights does the test give you?

* Talk with your pastor and church leaders about the possibility of offering more worship options. Try the congregational test in *Discover Your Spiritual Type*. Look around your community and talk with the unchurched about their needs. Study resources such as *Growing Spiritual Redwoods* and establish a design team to develop and implement some creative new experiences. Reassure long-time members that their needs will still be met, even as you reach out to others.

Prayer

O Holy Source of grace and power, breathe into me your love, that I may share that love with others. I thank you for the gift of the Holy Spirit and for all its manifestations in our lives. Forgive me for the times I am so distracted and dragged down that I ignore your calling and the wonderful possibilities available to me. Thank you for all who follow you faithfully and allow you to work through them. May their example and their support open me more fully to your purpose. In the name of Jesus, who obeyed you even to the point of death. Amen.

"I have said these things to you while I am still with you. But the Advocate, the Holy Spirit, whom the Father will send in my name, will teach you everything, and remind you of all that I have said to you." (John 14:25-26)

Maturing in Christ

F ROM THE TIME she was seventeen years old, Jane Griffith dreamed of becoming a missionary, but instead she went directly from nurse's training to marriage. She and Walter started a family, and she continued to practice her profession while raising their children. As she neared retirement, while taking part in a Disciple Bible study in her local church, she felt that mission dream return, stronger than before. Her husband, Walter, encouraged her to apply for an assignment and get it out of her system. Red Bird Mission accepted her, not for nursing but for a teaching role, which she thought she would dislike. However, upon her arrival at the center, she felt a strong conviction that she was in the right place. After she had been there two months, Walter came to visit and ended up finishing the school year there too, working maintenance and helping with Meals on Wheels. They both returned for several short terms during the next year and then decided to commit for a year after that.

This time Walter joined the work camp volunteers, and Jane served as a Christian education teacher, working in church

Therefore, my beloved, just as you have always obeyed me, not only in my presence, but much more now in my absence, work out your own salvation with fear and trembling; for it is God who is at work in you, enabling you both to will and to work for his good pleasure.
—Philippians 2:12-13

outreach for the conference as well. Walter's mother came along too, spending much of her time trimming, counting, and tying up soup labels, redeemable for school equipment, that had been donated to the mission.

Referring to a poster at Red Bird Mission, Jane quoted, "If you find yourself in a place you never thought you'd be and doing things you never thought you'd do, you can be sure that it's God's will!" Jane added, "I never thought I'd find myself in front of a class, with all those eager little faces. It was just God and me and the kids—the first time I ever felt God using me so. You could see the impact on the children of being in a Christian school, God breaking through in ways you think are impossible and reaching people you don't think can be reached." Rather than getting the missionary dream out of her system, Jane and Walter both were transformed by short-term mission work. "Now we continue our fellowship in the church here, studying the scriptures while waiting and listening for the next call and the next blessings God has planned for us."

Jeff Toothaker recalled his first mission trip to Nicaragua: "There were several times during the week when tears came to my eyes, both tears of joy and tears of sadness. At one point early in the week, I had seen so much destruction from the 1972 earthquake. I had seen shacks built in the shadow of destroyed buildings. I saw children on the street selling whatever they could or asking for money. As we came to a stoplight, there was a girl, probably about ten years old, holding her toddler sister. I thought of my own children and, as a jet flew over, I thought, 'OK, Lord, I've seen enough. Put me on that jet and take me home.' But I had been sent here, and there were many gifts and opportunities ahead of me during the week. I returned home with increased gratitude for all that we have, for the work of the church both here and in Nicaragua, and for faith that can provide strength for the journey, especially during severe hardships. I feel challenged to share the love of God in all the ways I can and to continue to put my faith into action. My first Sunday back at my home church, I heard people talk of supporting one another during times of sickness and death and reaching out to a church whose building had burned down, and I had a deeper sense of these involvements as mission. Let's all be in mission wherever we can, opening our arms and saying freely, with Isaiah, 'Here am I! Send me.'"

Whether or not we continue to participate in mission projects, as do the Griffiths, Jeff, and many other volunteers, our sense of vocation may be reshaped by a deeper understanding of mission and the knowledge of how we can make a difference. Audrey Stanton explained, "People hear the word *missionary* and think of someone preaching about God; but when I went to Africa University, I was with people who already know and follow Jesus. My mission was not to preach but to build shelves and work on housing and use my journalism skills to assist people. By helping Africa University provide education for students from all over the continent, I can help all of Africa move toward a better quality of life."

Volunteers returning from short-term mission projects may also demonstrate changed attitudes and behaviors. A pastor told me that a girl in his church has seemed much more outgoing and at ease in relationships since returning from her trip. Parents of youth who worked on an inner-city project reported that their sons and daughters no longer go to the refrigerator and mumble disgustedly, "There's nothing to eat." A high school senior on our Africa University team exclaimed, "I'll never complain about having to go to school again!" Witnessing genuine physical hunger, as well as the longing for education expressed by those without easy access to schools, confronts us with the reality of our privileged status.

Dr. John Claypool, after exploring a variety of reasons why the Samaritan may have stopped to help the wounded man on the Jericho road, revealed his own crisis of faith, one that occurred when his daughter was diagnosed with leukemia. The story of Abraham and Isaac, reinterpreted for him as a test of Abraham's understanding of life as a gift, rather than as a right, startled him out of despair. He learned to cultivate gladness for his daughter's having been part of their family, rather than focusing on the brevity of her life. Dr. Claypool suggests that Good Samaritan-like acts of kindness are most properly motivated by awareness that all of life is a gift.[13] Participation in short-term mission projects can nurture in us an "attitude of gratitude," as opposed to the belief that we are entitled to the blessings and benefits of our particular life.

In addition, we expand our understanding of God's power at work in the world, and we discover that power enabling our adjustment to unfamiliar and even uncomfortable circumstances. We experience time as a gift, rather than a burden. We recognize Jesus in the faces of new friends and colleagues. We learn what it means to live in Christian community. Corporately and privately, we experience more deeply God's presence in our lives, teaching, leading, healing. And we understand our utter dependence on God's grace to free us from sin and move us toward wholeness.

Justo González points out that when Jesus called the fishermen at the Sea of Galilee, he not only persuaded them "to follow him but also to redefine and recreate their lives."[14] That kind of spiritual growth requires more than the acquisition of new information. Through hands-on experiences and intensive relationships, God can most effectively chip away whatever is less than God's intention for us. Keith Miller, who has experienced personal transformation through Twelve Step groups, compares this to the work of a sculptor who trims away stone to find a beautiful statue waiting to be revealed, noting that "although the emerging person has always been there inside us waiting to be released, to be reborn, the feeling is that we are new people, new creations. And we finally see that just as God made us to be—we are enough."[15]

Indeed, God's vision of shalom for us as individuals, as well as for the entire creation, seems best summed up in the great commandment, as stated by Jesus: "'You shall love the Lord your God with all your heart, and with all your soul, and with all your mind.' This is the greatest and first commandment.

And a second is like it: 'You shall love your neighbor as your-self'" (Matt. 22:37-39). Love is not just a feeling. In the words of Hannah Hurnard, love is "an overmastering passion to help and bless and deliver and comfort and strengthen and give joy to others just as the Lord Jesus always did."[16] Even as we hold this vision firmly before us as a goal for growth, we may also embrace it as a possibility now, for each moment and encounter of each and every day.

So if anyone is in Christ, there is a new creation: everything old has passed away; see, everything has become new! (2 Cor. 5:17)

Reflection
- What changes in yourself, in your attitudes and perspectives, please you most?
- What changes have been most difficult?
- In what ways do you hope to continue to grow and change?
- What can you do to facilitate such growth?

Response
- Read back through the journal you began while preparing for your mission project. Highlight those entries or comments that indicate new insights or deeper spiritual awareness.
- Consider with whom and how you can share these personal reflections. If you are not part of an ongoing covenant prayer group, perhaps you could get together with other mission volunteers or other church friends to process the changes you have experienced. See pages 161–63 for covenant group guidelines and other spiritual growth resources.

Prayer

Holy, merciful God, I know that we have only just begun. I praise and thank you for my whole journey, for all that has brought me to where I am today. I also praise and thank you for whatever lies ahead. As I place myself in your loving hands, help me to do your will with joy. In the name of Jesus, whose resurrection reveals your power and promises infinite possibilities for our lives. Amen.

Beloved, we are God's children now; what we will be has not yet been revealed. What we do know is this: when he is revealed, we will be like him, for we will see him as he is. (1 John 3:2)

Resources

ORGANIZATIONAL HELPS FOR TEAM LEADERS

**Mission Volunteer Office,
United Methodist Church**
This office of The General Board of Global
Ministries of The United Methodist Church
resources Volunteer in Mission programs,
both for teams and for individuals.
Coordinating with all five jurisdictional
offices and linking with mission agencies to
determine their needs, this office provides
manuals, lists of projects and opportunities,
and specific helps.

   Mission Volunteer Office, United
Methodist Church, 475 Riverside Drive,
Room 330, New York, NY 10115
   Phone: 212-870-3825
   Fax: 212-870-3624
   E-mail: Voluntrs@gbgm-umc.org
   Web site: http://gbgm-umc.org/vim

Handbook for United Methodist Volunteers in Mission
United Methodist Volunteers in Mission
Southeastern Jurisdiction Office of Coordination

This handbook contains general information for short-term mission volunteer teams and specific information for international adult teams, international adult medical teams, youth and college teams, and disaster response teams. Guidelines and helpful suggestions for obtaining sponsorship, selecting projects, and recruiting team members are provided, along with important information on a variety of topics, sample worksheets, and worship resources. A few examples: budget preparation, packing donated items and supplies to facilitate getting through customs, immunization and prophylactic medications, insurance, and a "Checklist As I Face a New Culture."

Order from United Methodist Volunteers in Mission, Southeastern Jurisdiction Office of Coordination, 159 Ralph McGill Boulevard, NE, #305, Atlanta, GA 30308-3353.

Phone: 404-659-5060; fax: 404-659-2977
E-mail: sejumvim@compuserve.com
Web site: http://www.gbgm-umc.org/Volunteers

Appalachia Service Project, Inc.

ASP provides opportunities for Christian mission through a ministry of home repair and rehabilitation and new home construction in Central Appalachia. In addition to an eight-week summer ministry, ASP has three year-round centers and a staff to coordinate projects and provide informational and training programs, as well as service opportunities for youth, college-aged, and adult groups.

Appalachia Service Project, Inc., 4523 Bristol Highway, Johnson City, TN 37601

Phone: 423-854-8800; fax: 423-854-9771
E-mail: asp@asphome.org
Web site: http://www.asphome.org

Habitat for Humanity

This office provides technical support to local affiliate groups, which utilize volunteers in construction projects to eliminate substandard housing. Their work is based on a belief that every one who lies down to sleep at night should have a safe and comfortable place to do so.

To find out about projects in your area, contact the Habitat for Humanity International Headquarters, 121 Habitat Street, Americus, GA 31709.

Phone: 800-422-4828; fax: 912-924-6541
E-mail: public_info@habitat.org
Web site: http://www.habitat.org

Society of St. Andrew

This organization offers resources for spiritual growth and mission education, as well as specific instructions for organizing gleaning events to salvage surplus food for distribution to the poor.

For further information and an updated Resource Order Form, contact the Society of St. Andrew, 3383 Sweet Hollow Road, Big Island, VA 24526-3054.

Phone: 804-299-5956; 800-333-4597
Fax: 804-299-5949; E-mail: sosausa@mindspring.com
Web site: http://www.endhunger.org

Reach Workcamps

This nonprofit organization offers quality workcamp experiences and actively encourages workcamp participants to adopt a lifestyle of serving those in need in their home communities.

For further information write Reach Workcamps, Box 1614, Loveland, CO 80539.

Phone: 888-REACH-WC
Fax: 970-667-0598; E-mail: reachwc@info2000.net
Web site: http://www.reachwc.org

COMMISSIONING AND OTHER WORSHIP IDEAS

Commissioning, consecration, or dedication services for mission work teams should take place within the community of faith represented by the participants. Conference-wide teams may be commissioned in annual conference settings. Cooperative parish or local church teams may be dedicated in services involving members of those groups. If the commissioning is held within an already scheduled service or event, not only are more persons likely to be present, but more importantly, the work team project is celebrated as part of the ongoing life of the church.

The Southeastern Jurisdiction's *Handbook for United Methodist Volunteers in Mission*, described on page 150, contains a simple liturgy for such a service, as well as two other creative rituals. Any of these ceremonies, "Service of Sending Forth," "The Covenant of the Salt," and "The Peace Candle Ceremony," could be incorporated into commissioning services or used on other occasions, such as rallies or reunions of work team participants.

At the very least, commissioning services should include an opening statement explaining the purpose of the project, a challenge to the participants, and a response by the community of faith. The opening statement might include words of Jesus, such as John 15:9; John 15:16; and Mark 16:15. A brief general statement on mission, perhaps from denominational resources, could be followed by a few sentences about the specific destination of the team or teams being commissioned.

A simple challenge to team members is provided in the Southeastern Jurisdiction's service (*Handbook*, 59):

> "Do you sincerely believe that you have been led by the Spirit of God to engage in this ministry?" (Response: "I do so believe.")
>
> "Will you earnestly seek to carry forward this mission in a Christ-like manner, in cooperation with your fellow

team members and leader, and in full respect of the national church officials and local hosts?" (Response: "I will, the Lord being my helper.)

Team members could then be invited to kneel while the minister and congregation pray for them to receive God's blessings, guidance, and strength, as well as traveling mercies and openness to new understandings. The team and the congregation could then sing together a relevant hymn, such as "Here I Am, Lord" or "This Is My Song."

The *United Methodist Book of Worship* also includes "An Order for Commissioning to Short-Term Christian Service," page 592, which uses the World Methodist Social Affirmation (*United Methodist Hymnal*, 886) or an abbreviated version of The United Methodist Social Creed.

Worship should be an integral part of the team's experience, not just an activity structured for specific times and places. Responsibility for table grace may be rotated among the members, providing opportunity for a variety of forms, ranging from singing the doxology to the offering of extemporaneous prayers. During team meetings, reporting in on the day's experiences may be incorporated into shared prayer. As each person lifts up a joy or concern for the day, the group may respond, "Lord, in your mercy, hear our prayer." In similar fashion, members may be invited to tell about something good that happened to them that day, with the group responding, "Thanks be to God." A rousing chorus of "This Is the Day" (*United Methodist Hymnal*, 657) would serve as an effective morning wake-up call. Many tasks, such as passing bricks from person to person, can be set to the music of familiar hymns, lifting up the holy in the midst of common labor. Particular mission sites offer unique opportunities to include in team worship indigenous symbols and rituals, such as songs learned from the hosts, African drums, or the prayer candles of Russian Orthodox churches.

Most team members already have favorite hymns that will quickly become part of the team's tradition. The following list includes some that are particularly meaningful during mission projects. The numbers given are from *Global Praise* (GP), *Praise: Maranatha! Music Chorus Book* (CB), and *The United Methodist Hymnal* (UMH), with bibliographical information on those sources at the end of this section. Most of these songs, however, may also be found in other songbooks and denominational resources:

Finding God Already at Work
"Christ for the World We Sing" (UMH, 568)
"For the Healing of the Nations" (UMH, 428)
"Here I Am, Lord" (UMH, 593)
"Let There Be Peace on Earth" (UMH, 431)
"Lord, Whose Love through Humble Service" (UMH, 581)
"Lord, You Give the Great Commission" (UMH, 584)
"The Right Hand of God" (GP, 60)
"We Are Standing on Holy Ground" (CB, 225)
"We've a Story to Tell to the Nations" (UMH, 569)
"Where Cross the Crowded Ways of Life" (UMH, 427)

Experiencing Hospitality
"Freely, Freely" (UMH, 389; CB, 263)
"When the Poor Ones Who Have Nothing" (UMH, 434)

Making Adjustments
"Amazing Grace" (UMH, 378)
"How Firm a Foundation" (UMH, 529)
"It Is Well with My Soul" (UMH, 377)
"It's Me, It's Me, O Lord" (UMH, 352)
"Leaning on the Everlasting Arms" (UMH, 133)
"Saranam, Saranam" (UMH, 523)
"John 16:33 (These Things Have I Spoken unto You)" (CB, 198)
"This Little Light of Mine" (UMH, 585)

"Turn Your Eyes Upon Jesus" (UMH, 349; CB, 97)
"O Master, Let Me Walk with Thee" (UMH, 430)

Liberating Time

"Dear Jesus in Whose Life I See" (UMH, 468)
"Great Is Thy Faithfulness" (UMH, 140)
"Let It Breathe on Me" (UMH, 503)
"Lord of the Dance" (UMH, 261)
"Take My Life, and Let It Be" (UMH, 399)
"'Tis So Sweet to Trust in Jesus" (UMH, 462)
"This Is the Day" (UMH, 657; CB, 85)
"Through It All" (UMH, 507)
"Trust and Obey" (UMH, 467)

Meeting Jesus

"Make Me a Servant" (CB, 177)
"O Many People of All Lands" (GP, 51)
"The Servant Song" (CB, 205)
"There's a Wideness in God's Mercy" (UMH, 121)
"We Meet You, O Christ" (UMH, 257)
"Shalom to You" (UMH, 666)

Building a Team

"Bind Us Together" (CB, 73)
"Blest Be the Tie That Binds" (UMH, 557)
"Dame la Mano" ("Give Me Your Hand") (GP, 18)
"Help Us Accept Each Other" (UMH, 560)
"Jesus, United by Thy Grace" (UMH, 561)

Singing the Lord's Song

"Alleluia" (UMH, 186)
"Alleluia, Alleluia" (UMH, 162)
"All Praise to Our Redeeming Lord" (UMH, 554)
"Breathe on Me, Breath of God" (UMH, 420)
"Cantemos al Señor" ("Let's Sing unto the Lord")
    (UMH, 149)

"God of Many Names" (UMH, 105)
"Halleluja" (GP, 31)
"Jesu Tawa Pano" ("Jesus, We Are Here") (GP, 36)
"Surely the Presence of the Lord Is in This Place"
    (UMH, 328; CB, 233)
"What a Mighty God We Serve" (CB, 132)

Maturing in Christ

"I Am Thine, O Lord" (UMH, 419)
"On Eagle's Wings" (UMH, 143)
"Seek Ye First" (UMH, 405; CB, 1)
"Spirit of the Living God" (UMH, 393; CB, 82)
"The Gift of Love" (UMH, 408)

Kimbrough, S. T., Jr., and Carlton R. Young. *Global Praise 1.* New York: General Board of Global Ministries, GBGMusik, rev., 1997.
Praise: Maranatha! Music Chorus Book. Nashville, Tenn.: The Benson Co., Inc., 1990.
The United Methodist Hymnal. Nashville, Tenn.: The United Methodist Publishing House, 1989.

SUGGESTIONS FOR GROUP USE OF THIS GUIDE

Part One: Before You Leave Home

If team members have been asked to complete Part One before leaving home, discussion of the material might take place during a team meeting prior to departure, using the following questions:

- Have you already had any experiences similar to those described in Part One?

- What stories, themes, or issues surprised you?

- What suggestions did you find most helpful?

- What made you uncomfortable?

- What have you done differently because of using this material?

- What did you learn about yourself?

- What are your hopes for this experience? fears?

- What do you anticipate you will need from your teammates?

- What did you learn from your other reading about our mission site?

After others have shared, the team leader may want to relate some experiences and insights of his or her own, as well as select some of the Reflection questions for group discussion. If the team meets several times before departure, there will, of course, be more time for such discussion.

Part Two: During Your Mission Project

If it is not possible to schedule enough team meeting time to deal with all eight theme chapters, select those you want to use with the group and ask team members to use the others privately or in small groups. For each group session, team members will need their copies of this book, their Bibles, their journals, and pens or pencils. Select from the following suggestions what you can reasonably complete during the allotted time, encouraging members to do the rest on their own.

Have someone read the scripture passage aloud, while the rest of the members follow along in their own Bibles. Note that passages quoted in this book are from the New Revised Standard Version. If team members have different translations, you might ask them to share any significant differences. Help bring the scripture to life by asking members to name words that jump out at them from the passage, then to describe mental pictures associated with it, including any related sounds or smells.

Assign someone ahead of time to read and prepare a summary of the commentary.

Discuss both sets of Reflection questions as a group.

Give time for the team members to sit quietly and get in touch with their feelings about the scripture passage. Invite them to write in their journals as if they were talking to God about it. Tell them that they will be asked to share only what they choose.

Form pairs or groups of three, directing members to take turns sharing whatever they choose from what they have written. Alternatively, a small team might try "Conversation by Mutual Invitation," described below.

Give team members time now or encourage them to take time later to sit quietly and listen for God's guidance, recording in their journals any thoughts or impressions that come.

Direct team members to read through the suggested Responses. Ask for discussion or questions.

Close with prayer.

Conversation by Mutual Invitation

This process for discussion, from Eric Law's *The Wolf Shall Dwell with the Lamb*, may seem awkward at first but can be a powerful instrument for facilitating openness and group sharing. Whatever the topic, the leader begins by explaining that this procedure makes sure everyone who wants to share has the opportunity to do so.

The leader or other designated person speaks first in response to a question or topic. When finished, he or she invites another person to share, preferably not someone in the next seat. The invited person then shares or says "pass" and invites someone else to share next. The process continues until all have been invited to share. It may be necessary, at first, to remind each speaker to invite the next. You might want to read Eric Law's book to understand fully the rationale and impact of this process.[1]

Part Three: After Your Return

If you can convene a group that has read some or all of the theme chapters in Part Three, you might use "Conversation by Mutual Invitation" as described above or simply discuss the following questions:

- What stories, themes, or issues in Part Three had the most impact on you?

- What suggestions did you find most helpful?
- What made you uncomfortable?
- What have you done differently because of using this material?
- What are you learning about yourself?
- What are your hopes for continued growth? fears?
- What support do you need? Where can you find that support?

SUGGESTIONS FOR FOLLOW-UP STUDY

Understanding Racism and Multicultural Issues

First We Must Listen: Living in a Multicultural Society, edited by Anne Leo Ellis (New York: Friendship Press,1996).
Leader's Guide to *First We Must Listen: Living in a Multicultural Society*, by Marilyn Winters (New York: Friendship Press, 1996).

This study is based on the premise "that in order to dissolve the barriers separating us, we must first be willing to listen: to attend carefully and compassionately to the pain and anger, the frustration and dismay of those who have suffered the blows and dislocations of racial and ethnic hatred. At the same time we are enjoined to fully appreciate the beauty and strength, the variety and richness that each culture brings to our collective party—our 'incredible mosaic,' in the words of one contributor."[2] The readings in the study text vividly present a variety of experiences and points of view. The study guide offers plans for six sessions with alternatives for a variety of schedules and settings.

Stewardship

Curing Affluenza. (Nashville, Tenn.: UMCOM Productions, 1998). Available from EcuFilm, 810 Twelfth Ave. So., Nashville, TN 37203. 800-251-4091; www.ecuFilm.org.

This six-session study includes six 20- to 25-minute videos featuring Tony Campolo, along with a comprehensive study guide. Focused on how to simplify our lives in order to live more fully, it addresses issues related to money, time, and possessions.

Living Simply, Simply Living, by Delia Halverson (Nashville, Tenn.: Abingdon Press, 1996).

This book offers "practical suggestions for taking steps to simplify your life," with the specific focus on moving closer to God and God's direction for your life.[3] Action plans and charts, as well as the text itself, would be useful for personal reflection. A study guide for six group sessions is included at the end of the book.

'Tis a Gift to Be Simple: Embracing the Freedom of Living with Less, by Barbara DeGrote-Sorensen and David Allen Sorensen (Minneapolis, Minn.: Augsburg Fortress, 1992).

This book relates the authors' attempts to simplify their lifestyle in order to "hear God speaking to us."[4] The authors provide six weeks of daily scripture selections and prayers for reflection on simplicity.

Team Building and Interpersonal Relationships

Parent Effectiveness Training: The "No-Lose" Program for Raising Responsible Children, by Thomas Gordon (New York: Peter H. Wyden, Inc., 1970).

This book presents clear explanations and useful illustrations of effective communication and conflict management skills. The same concepts applied in different contexts are presented in Dr. Gordon's later books: *T.E.T.: Teacher Effectiveness Training* (New York: Peter H. Wyden, 1974) and *Leader Effectiveness Training (L.E.T.): The No-Lose Way to Release the Productive Potential of People* (New York: Bantam Books, 1977).

Partners in Ministry: Clergy and Laity, by Roy W. Trueblood and Jackie B. Trueblood (Nashville: Abingdon Press, 1999).

This book outlines a process designed to help clergy and lay leadership work together more effectively. Clear statements of the assumptions and ground rules necessary for true partnership are followed by discussion of interpersonal skills essential for application of the process.

Community Transformation

Communities of Shalom (475 Riverside Drive, Room 1545, New York, NY 10115. Phone: 212-870-3832)

The Communities of Shalom concept is designed to enable the help, hope, and healing needed by congregations and neighborhoods to address both the internal and external pressures of poverty, racism, lack of vision, lack of resources, and spiritual decline. This program provides training, follow-up support, and technical assistance to help groups strategize for church and community transformation. Clergy, laity, community leaders, and residents learn planning and leadership skills. An initiative of The United Methodist Church, coordinated by the General Board of Global Ministries in consultation with the National Shalom Committee, this program involves five full-day training sessions over a five-month period of time. To participate, annual conferences must have three to seven potential Communities of Shalom teams, each involving eight to twenty church and community participants willing to commit to the entire training process.

Personal Spiritual Growth

Covenant Groups

Gwen White shares the following guidelines for covenant groups, a disciplined way of being together that enriches and deepens the members' faith and relationships. The groups meet once a month and require from three to eight members, to allow everyone adequate sharing time. Since members take turns serving as facilitator and time-keeper, there is no need for a designated leader. Members agree on a devotional book, which they use daily during the month and bring to the meeting, along with their Bibles. Throughout the month the members feel connected by using the same devotional material while apart from each other.

Rueben Job and Norman Shawchuck have developed two devotional books (*A Guide to Prayer for Ministers and Other Servants* [Nashville, Tenn.: The Upper Room, 1983] and *A Guide to Prayer for All God's People* [Nashville, Tenn.: Upper Room Books, 1990], which work well for covenant groups. Both use the same format but with different content. For each week, a different theme is developed through prayers, daily scripture selections, a hymn, and gleanings from sacred writings by many different authors.

When the group gathers for its monthly meeting, preferably at the same time and place each month, the facilitator leads the members through the following process:

1. Five minutes of silence allow for centering and becoming present to God and one another.
2. The facilitator offers a prayer.
3. The members share which of the scriptures and other devotional materials spoke to them in a meaningful way, connected with their journeys, or provided new insights.
4. Members may then share more about their personal journeys, current struggles, joys, sorrows, or concerns. Confidentiality and trust are essential elements of covenantal relationships.
5. For closure, each member offers a single word for the others to use as a daily intercessory prayer on his or her behalf during the coming month. The use of these words—such as, *patience, strength, compassion, discernment*—makes it possible for the members to pray for one another in a specific way.

Resources

6. The group forms a prayer circle, and the facilitator prays for any who might be absent and for the person on his or her right. Each member, in turn, prays for the one on the right until all have been prayed for.

Covenant groups provide an excellent opportunity for volunteers to continue the spiritual growth they have experienced during short-term mission projects.

Covenant Discipleship and Class Leaders

Materials offered through this Christian formation program include *Covenant Discipleship: Christian Formation through Mutual Accountability; Class Leaders: Recovering a Tradition;* and *Forming Christian Disciples: The Role of Covenant Discipleship and Class Leaders in the Congregation,* written by David Lowes Watson. To order call toll-free at 800-865-4370; fax: 770-442-9742; order online at www.discipleshipresources.org; or mail to Discipleship Resources Distribution Center, P.O. Box 1616, Alpharetta, GA 30009-1616.

For program information about Covenant Discipleship and Class Leaders, contact the Director of Covenant Discipleship and Class Leaders, The General Board of Discipleship, P. O. Box 340003, Nashville, TN 37203-0003.

The Walk to Emmaus

Emmaus offers three-day events and follow-up experiences for developing Christian leaders who want to expand their inner spiritual life and become more active disciples of Christ in the world through the church. To find an Emmaus community near you, contact the Director of The Walk to Emmaus, The Upper Room, 1908 Grand Avenue, Nashville, TN 37212; emmaus@upperroom.org.

The Academy for Spiritual Formation

The Academy for Spiritual Formation offers intensive study programs at various locations for both lay and clergy who sense a call to a spiritually focused personal ministry and wish

163

to give significant priority to personal spiritual growth. Contact the Director of The Academy for Spiritual Formation, The Upper Room, 1908 Grand Avenue, Nashville, TN 37212.

For this reason I bow my knees before the Father, from whom every family in heaven and on earth takes its name. I pray that, according to the riches of his glory, he may grant that you may be strengthened in your inner being with power through his Spirit, and that Christ may dwell in your hearts through faith, as you are being rooted and grounded in love. I pray that you may have the power to comprehend, with all the saints, what is the breadth and length and height and depth, and to know the love of Christ that surpasses knowledge, so that you may be filled with all the fullness of God. Now to him who by the power at work within us is able to accomplish abundantly far more than all we can ask or imagine, to him be glory in the church and in Christ Jesus to all generations, forever and ever. Amen. (Eph. 3:14-21)

164

Notes

Part One: Before You Leave Home

1. Thomas Moore, *The Re-Enchantment of Everyday Life* (New York: HarperCollins, Inc., 1996), 139.
2. Sally Campbell-Evans, *People, Places and Partnerships: A Workbook for Your Mission Trip Abroad* (Louisville, Ky.: Presbyterian Church [USA], 1996), 37.
3. Robert Brizee, *Where in the World Is God? God's Presence in Every Moment of Our Lives* (Nashville, Tenn.: The Upper Room, 1987), 62.
4. Ibid., 133.
5. Elisha A. Hoffman, "Leaning on the Everlasting Arms," *The United Methodist Hymnal* (Nashville, Tenn.: The United Methodist Publishing House, 1989), 133.
6. Raymond K. DeHainaut, "Cross-Cultural Spirituality for Volunteers in Mission," *New World Outlook* (September–October 1995): 18.
7. Moore, *The Re-Enchantment*, 5.
8. *United Methodist Hymnal*, 657; *Praise: Maranatha! Music Chorus Book* (Nashville, Tenn.: The Benson Company, Inc., 1990), 85.
9. Frances R. Havergal, "Take My Life, and Let It Be," *The United Methodist Hymnal*, 399.
10. John Wesley, *The Works of John Wesley*, vol. 3, edited by Albert C. Outler, (Nashville, Tenn.: Abingdon Press, 1986), 387.
11. Ambrose Reeves, *Calvary Now* (London: SCM Press, 1965), 77.
12. Mother Teresa, *No Greater Love* (Novato, Calif.: New World Library, 1997), 84–85.
13. Hannah Hurnard, *Hinds' Feet on High Places* (Wheaton, Ill.: Tyndale House Publishers, 1975), 198, 211–14.

14. Keith Miller, *A Hunger for Healing: The Twelve Steps as a Classic Model for Christian Spiritual Growth* (San Franciso: HarperSanFrancisco, 1991), 6.

Part Two: During Your Mission Project

1. David J. Lawson, *Hungering for the Future: Whispers of Hope for a Church in Mission* (Nashville, Tenn.: Abingdon Press, 1996), 152–54.

2. *Dictionary of the Bible*, rev. ed., edited by Frederick C. Grant and H. H. Rowley (New York: Charles Scribner's Sons, 1963), 399–401.

3. Moore, *The Re-Enchantment*, 148.

4. M. Robert Mulholland Jr., "Expecting the Unexpected," *The Upper Room Disciplines 1997* (Nashville, Tenn.: The Upper Room, 1996), 365, 366.

5. *The Interpreter's Bible*, vol. 9, edited by George A. Buttrick (Nashville, Tenn.: Abingdon Press, 1954), 131–134, 142.

6. Ibid., 198–99.

7. Reeves, *Calvary Now*, 77.

8. Campbell-Evans, *People, Places and Partnerships*, 29.

9. *The Interpreter's Bible*, vol. 11, edited by George A. Buttrick (Nashville, Tenn.: Abingdon Press, 1955), 218.

10. Ibid., 218–222.

11. *The Interpreter's Bible*, vol. 4, edited by George A. Buttrick (Nashville: Abingdon Press, 1955), 532–34.

12. *Dictionary of the Bible*, 1044.

13. Robert E. Webber, *Worship Is a Verb: Eight Principles for a Highly Participatory Worship* (Nashville, Tenn.: Abbott Martyn, 1992), 206–207.

14. Corinne Ware, *Discover Your Spiritual Type: A Guide to Individual and Congregational Growth* (Bethesda, Md.: The Alban Institute, 1995), 102–107.

15. *The Interpreter's Bible*, vol. 4, 266–67.

16. Ibid., 268–270.

17. Saint John of the Cross, *Dark Night of the Soul* (New York: Image Books, 1959), 127–29.

18. "K" in Rippon's *A Selection of Hymns,* 1787 (2 Tim. 2:19; Heb. 13:5; Isa. 43:1-2).

Part Three: After Your Return

1. Moore, *The Re-enchantment*, 152.

2. Donella Meadows, "How Big a House Does a Person Need?" *The Charleston* (West Virginia) *Gazette*, 5 January 1998, A8.

3. Siang-Yang Tan and Douglas H. Gregg, *Disciplines of the Holy Spirit: How to Connect with the Spirit's Power and Presence* (Grand Rapids, Mich.: ZondervanPublishingHouse, 1997), 130–132, 138, 139.

4. Justo L. González, *When Christ Lives in Us: A Pilgrimage of Faith* (Nashville, Tenn.: Abingdon Press, 1995), 60, 14.

5. T. C. Whitehouse, "Journal Jottings," *Cross Currents/Zion's Herald* (22 December 1997): 29.

6. John Claypool, "Witness and Proclamation: How We Can Make Our Sorrows Sing," audiotape of lecture presented in the *Newscope* Lecture Series, March 1989 (Nashville, Tenn.: United Methodist Publishing House, 1989).

7. Helen and Scott Nearing, *The Good Life* (New York: Schocken Books, 1989), 388–89.

8. Boyce A. Boyden, "Sharing God's Love in Bosnia," *New World Outlook* (November–December 1996), 17.

9. William M. Easum and Thomas G. Bandy, *Growing Spiritual Redwoods* (Nashville, Tenn.: Abingdon Press, 1997), 65–66.

10. Ware, *Spiritual Type*, 28, 36–45.

11. Sarah Ban Breathnach, *Simple Abundance: A Daybook of*

Comfort and Joy (New York: Warner Books, 1995), February 11.

12. Tan and Gregg, *Disciplines*, 8, 9.
13. Claypool, "Witness and Proclamation."
14. González, *When Christ Lives in Us*, 11.
15. Miller, *Hunger for Healing*, 216–217.
16. Hurnard, *Hinds' Feet*, 294.

Resources

1. Eric H. F. Law, *The Wolf Shall Dwell with the Lamb: A Spirituality for Leadership in a Multicultural Community* (St. Louis, Mo.: Chalice Press, 1993), 113,114.
2. Anne Leo Ellis, ed., *First We Must Listen: Living in a Multicultural Society* (New York: Friendship Press, 1996), back cover.
3. Delia Halverson, *Living Simply* (Nashville, Tenn.: Abingdon Press, 1996), back cover.
4. Barbara DeGrote-Sorensen and David Allen Sorensen, *'Tis a Gift to Be Simple: Embracing the Freedom of Living with Less* (Minneapolis, Minn.: Augsburg Fortress, 1992), back cover.

Works Cited

Boyden, Boyce A. "Sharing God's Love in Bosnia." *New World Outlook* (November–December 1996).

Breathnach, Sarah Ban. *Simple Abundance: A Daybook of Comfort and Joy.* New York: Warner Books, 1995.

Brizee, Robert. *Where in the World Is God? God's Presence in Every Moment of Our Lives.* Nashville, Tenn.: The Upper Room, 1987.

Buttrick, George A., ed. *The Interpreter's Bible*, vols. 4 and 11. Nashville, Tenn.: Abingdon Press, 1955.

_____. *The Interpreter's Bible*, vol. 9. Nashville, Tenn.: Abingdon Press, 1954.

Campbell-Evans, Sally. *People, Places and Partnerships: A Workbook for Your Mission Trip Abroad.* Louisville, Ky.: Presbyterian Church (USA), 1996.

Claypool, John. "Witness and Proclamation: How We Can Make Our Sorrows Sing," audiotape of lecture presented in the Newscope Lecture Series, March 1989 (Nashville, Tenn.: United Methodist Publishing House, 1989).

DeGrote-Sorensen, Barbara, and David Allen Sorensen. *'Tis a Gift to Be Simple: Embracing the Freedom of Living with Less.* Minneapolis, Minn.: Augsburg Fortress, 1992.

DeHainaut, Raymond K. "Cross-Cultural Spirituality for Volunteers in Mission." *New World Outlook* (September–October 1995).

Easum, William M,. and Thomas G. Bandy. *Growing Spiritual Redwoods.* Nashville, Tenn.: Abingdon Press, 1997.

Ellis, Anne Leo, ed., *First We Must Listen: Living in a Multicultural Society,* Leader's Guide. Written by Marilyn Winters. New York: Friendship Press, 1996.

González, Justo L. *When Christ Lives in Us: A Pilgrimage of Faith.* Nashville, Tenn.: Abingdon Press, 1995.

Grant, Frederick C. and H. H. Rowley, eds. *Dictionary of the*

Bible, revised edition. New York: Charles Scribner's Sons, 1963.

Halverson, Delia. *Living Simply, Simply Living*. Nashville, Tenn.: Abingdon Press, 1996.

Hurnard, Hannah. *Hinds' Feet on High Places*. Wheaton, Ill.: Tyndale House Publishers, 1975.

Law, Eric H. F. *The Wolf Shall Dwell with the Lamb: A Spirituality for Leadership in a Multicultural Community*. St. Louis, Mo.: Chalice Press, 1993.

Lawson, David J. *Hungering for the Future: Whispers of Hope for a Church in Mission*. Nashville, Tenn.: Abingdon Press, 1996.

Meadows, Donella. "How Big a House Does a Person Need?" *The Charleston* (West Virginia) *Gazette*, 5 January 1998, A8.

Miller, Keith. *A Hunger for Healing: The Twelve Steps as a Classic Model for Christian Spiritual Growth*. San Franciso: HarperSanFrancisco, 1991.

Moore, Thomas. *The Re-Enchantment of Everyday Life*. New York: HarperCollins Publishers, Inc., 1996.

Mulholland, M. Robert, Jr. "Expecting the Unexpected." *The Upper Room Disciplines 1997*. Nashville, Tenn.: The Upper Room, 1996.

Nearing, Helen, and Scott. *The Good Life*. New York: Schocken Books, 1989.

Outler, Albert C., ed. *The Works of John Wesley*. Vol. 3. Nashville, Tenn.: Abingdon Press, 1986.

Reeves, Ambrose. *Calvary Now*. London: SCM Press, 1965.

Saint John of the Cross. *Dark Night of the Soul*. New York: Image Books, 1959.

Tan, Siang-Yang, and Douglas H. Gregg. *Disciplines of the Holy Spirit: How to Connect with the Spirit's Power and Presence*. Grand Rapids, Mich.: ZondervanPublishingHouse, 1997.

Teresa, Mother. *No Greater Love*. Novato, Calif.: New World Library, 1997.

The United Methodist Hymnal. Nashville, Tenn.: The United Methodist Publishing House, 1989.

United Methodist Volunteers in Mission. *Handbook*. Atlanta,

Ga.: Southeastern Jurisdiction Office.

Ware, Corinne. *Discover Your Spiritual Type: A Guide to Individual and Congregational Growth.* Bethesda, Md.: The Alban Institute, 1995.

Webber, Robert E. *Worship Is a Verb: Eight Principles for a Highly Participatory Worship.* Nashville, Tenn.: Abbott Martyn, 1992.

Whitehouse, T. C. "Journal Jottings," *Cross Currents/Zion's Herald* (22 December 1997).

Winters, Marilyn. Leader's Guide to *First We Must Listen: Living in a Multicultural Society.* New York: Friendship Press, 1996.

About the Author

Born in New Jersey, Jane grew up in Maine, graduating from the University of Maine in 1960. She taught English and later served as a Special Educator in public schools, earning her master's degree in Exceptionality at the University of Southern Maine in 1990.

Jane became active in The United Methodist Church as a youth. In her adult years, she has participated in United Methodist Women, Christian education, Schools of Christian Mission, substance abuse prevention, and marriage enrichment. Since moving to West Virginia in 1992, she has provided consultative support to local tutoring programs, worked as a contracted evaluator for the county school system, and served with various conference agencies and programs. She focuses primarily on ministries to families and children. Most recently she traveled to Kosovo with a team of bishops' spouses to learn how we can support the work of The United Methodist Committee on Relief there, especially in regard to the reopening of schools and meeting the needs of women and children traumatized by war.

Her first book, *Couples Who Care*, was published by Discipleship Resources in 1997, followed by *Couples Who Cope* in 1999.

Jane and her husband, Bishop S. Clifton Ives, have traveled extensively throughout the United States as well as abroad: as volunteers in mission to Haiti, Russia, and Africa; on episcopal visitations to Mexico, Angola, Korea, and Argentina. Their three grown children and five grandchildren all live in New England.